MCAT Planner

AXILOGY

A 24-hour Daily Planner

Published by Axilogy Consultants LLC.

ISBN: 153546416X
ISBN-13: 978-1535464161
Third Edition
Printed in the U.S.

More Information: For information about special discounts available for bulk purchases, sales promotions, fundraising and educational needs, contact sales at admin@axilogy.com. We have provided bulk MCAT planners for university programs, premedical advisors, and masters program.

Feedback: We welcome all s for the planner and can make adjustments for future students with your input. Please send your valuable feedback to admin@axilogy.com. If you find the planner helpful, please share this resource with your peers, on social media, and through a review on Amazon so we can continue to help students. If this planner is missing anything that we can provide, please let us know immediately and we will consider it. If we come to the conclusion that your should be added immediately, we will send you an updated copy within a week.

Disclaimer: The Medical College Admission Test® ("MCAT®") is a program of the Association of American Medical Colleges ("AAMC") and is not affiliated with Axilogy Consultants. Axilogy is a premedical and MCAT education company which provides early medical education courses, private MCAT coaching, and preparation books/planners. This planner does not replace the role of premedical counselors or MCAT programs. This planner should be used in addition to your MCAT programs to maintain consistency and motivation through-out the process of your MCAT preparations. The advice in this planner should be taken into consideration with the advice of your counselor and other MCAT resources. This planner allows you to begin your prep at any time in the year, but you must fill in the dates as you go in light of this. The resources of this planner are at the end in order to allow you to easily access your plan first. Please use the *Axilogy Premedical Student Planner* after the MCAT to receive planning assistance for medical school beyond the MCAT planner. We have condensed this planner as much as possible to allow it to be easily carried.

A Note From the CEO: This book is dedicated to the aspiring students who work day and night to make their dreams of assisting patients a reality, The MCAT is one of the most important tests you will take in your life. We are simply here to make sure the process to prepare for this exam goes smoothly. We wish you all the best in planning for the exam and hope you find the feedback and measures used in this planner to keep you on track helpful. Remember through all of this preparation, you will come out stronger, brighter, and more capable of achieving your dreams. In this process, remember to always stay relaxed, take your time, believe in yourself, reward yourself, sleep more, be selfish of your study time, and of course, be kind to yourself. - Amareen Dhaliwal

As airlines always say *"Put your oxygen mask on before assisting someone else"*.

Table of Contents

Planner Preparation	
1	Do not take the test until you've scored 515 on at least 3 practice tests
2	Use forums to gain advice no more than once a week - do not use them to gain stress or anxiety
3	Start early! Begin in Fall instead of January f possible
4	Focus on strategies that have been effective
5	Take practice tests with other students at least once
6	Try to write your own AAMC MCAT questions
7	Analyze Bloom's Taxonomy to see how MCQ questions are made
8	Be happy and satisfied at the end of the day no matter what happened
9	Prepare the planner the NIGHT BEFORE instead of a week in advance
10	Always hand write notes, NEVER type notes (more retention)
11	Always read books and questions printed except for simulation tests (faster)
12	Use printer paper for notes
13	Take notes in a concept map method
14	Do not take neat notes or use colors for your notes
15	Use multiple companies for material review - rely on question-heavy review
16	Keep journaling in the common mistake log to review mistakes
17	Focus on a different purpose for the MCAT to reduce anxiety i.e. study to become an MCAT Test writer or tutor rather than
18	Develop a natural flowing CARS strategy for 1 week before altering
19	Always check the answer after every question rather than every passage during the content review phase of your preparation (increases retention)
20	Search online for practice questions rather than textbooks in the topic you desire
21	Use premade MCAT quizlet sets daily in different subjects to gain exposure
22	Focus on the "because" and "since" explanations to learn rather than memorizing
23	Knowing content will only get you to a 500! You must learn test taking.
24	Rank questions on a "smiley face scale" or "fraction scale" based on how relevantly they answer the question stem (NOT how true they are)
25	Write out 1-59 or 1-53 and A B C D on note paper for your section exams before hand to get prepared and visualize getting every answer correct
26	Treat each question like a patient case - it is important and complex!
27	Read articles in subjects you consider boring to learn how to become interested in unique CARS passages
28	Never use the highlight function on exams (it slows you down)
29	Use earplugs not headphones or music when studying
30	Use 3-5 different study locations (must practice recall in multiple areas)
31	Simulate a practice full length multiple times to increase endurance
32	Sleep in if you can (increases retention)
33	Take brain boosters such as DHA and Bacopa for extra support
34	Only 20% of the MCAT is fact, the remaining is conceptual and analytical
35	Follow your schedule and don't waste time questioning it too much
36	Reread the checklist to make sure you've covered every topic
37	Stick formulas in common areas to review them often
38	Read about memorization as a science to discover more
39	Try chunking 3-4 items in a concept map at a time to memorize
40	Work on ways to mentally remove stress caused by the exam
41	You should not use the stress of failing to work hard
42	Have a loved one remind you that you can accomplish this every day
43	Set up a countdown clock
44	Learn to become obsessed with the exam so you enjoy it more
45	Find small ways to reward yourself that do not take time such as dancing in the bathroom or watching a comedy show before falling asleep
46	Don't get scared of practice tests, just use them as tools to fix your mistakes
47	You shouldn't be making the same mistake more than once. It means you are not reviewing properly.
48	If tired during exams, split it into 5 question blocks. Every 5 questions, take a 5 second breather and get back to work.
49	Eat long-lasting light food such as oatmeal during study time or practice intermittent fasting and limit food until later in the day.
50	Use your cursor to keep track of the passage
51	Learn to fake an interest in the passage if it seems difficult
52	Translate CARS passages into simpler phrases. Do not be afraid to be flexible with the interpretation if you cannot understand it.
53	Visualize everything, Especially CARS passages as stories in your head. Treat them like patient histories and try to get the main concepts out of it.
54	For all passages, practice writing notes in concept makes WHILE reading (ie don't look down)
55	Never skip your daily CARS passage or quick sheet review.
56	Use a log for CARS that explains why A B C D are right or wrong in a broad sense. Review it right before your next CARS passage.
57	Use a log for practice tests with 50 mistakes. Review all practice test logs before the following practice test.

Developing A General Plan		
	Option 1 (aim for 4-6 months out. If your practice scores reflect that you are not ready for your Option 1 test date, extend to your Option 2 test date. Decide based on having 515+ practice test scores and a desirable AAMC practice test)	Option 2 (always have an Option 2. It is always smarter to push back the test date but not recommended to take the test when you are not ready)
Official Start Date		
Official Test Date		
Goal Official MCAT Score (505-528)		
Goal Practice FL Score (Aim for 515+)		
Goal Number of Practice Exams (aim for 25-49)		
Days Spent on Practice Exams (#FL x1 or x1.5)		
Total Weeks to Prepare		
Total Days to Prepare (do not include off days)		
Days Spent on Content (subtract total days - of Fls x1 or x1.5)		
Average Time for "NonMCAT" Tasks on Weekdays		
Average Time for "NonMCAT" Tasks on Weekend days		
Average Hours to Study on Weekdays (minimum 2-6 hours)		
Average Hours to Study on Weekend days (minimum 6-15 hours)		
Average Sleep Hours (**always** sleep 7.5+ hours during MCAT prep)		
Daily Review Goals (we recommend for mornings: 1 CARS Passage, Review cheatsheets, 1 MCAT Quizlet Set, Review common mistakes, Formula review - paste in bathroom or pin near bed to enforce revision)		
Goal Number of Practice Material to Use		
Non-MCAT Priorities (limit to 0-4 a week)		
Fitness Goals (loose weight, gain weight, same weight, gain muscle)		
Total Hours to Prepare (24 - Sleep hours - NonMCAT hours)xWeekdays + (24- Sleep hours - NonMCAT hours)xWeekend days		

Writing A General Plan

Date	Plan	Date	Plan	Date	Plan	Date	Plan	Date	Plan	Date	Plan	Date	Plan	Date	Plan
1		45		89		133		177		221		265		309	
2		46		90		134		178		222		266		310	
3		47		91		135		179		223		267		311	
4		48		92		136		180		224		268		312	
5		49		93		137		181		225		269		313	
6		50		94		138		182		226		270		314	
7		51		95		139		183		227		271		315	
8		52		96		140		184		228		272		316	
9		53		97		141		185		229		273		317	
10		54		98		142		186		230		274		318	
11		55		99		143		187		231		275		319	
12		56		100		144		188		232		276		320	
13		57		101		145		189		233		277		321	
14		58		102		146		190		234		278		322	
15		59		103		147		191		235		279		323	
16		60		104		148		192		236		280		324	
17		61		105		149		193		237		281		325	
18		62		106		150		194		238		282		326	
19		63		107		151		195		239		283		327	
20		64		108		152		196		240		284		328	
21		65		109		153		197		241		285		329	
22		66		110		154		198		242		286		330	
23		67		111		155		199		243		287		331	
24		68		112		156		200		244		288		332	
25		69		113		157		201		245		289		333	
26		70		114		158		202		246		290		334	
27		71		115		159		203		247		291		335	
28		72		116		160		204		248		292		336	
29		73		117		161		205		249		293		337	
30		74		118		162		206		250		294		338	
31		75		119		163		207		251		295		339	
32		76		120		164		208		252		296		340	
33		77		121		165		209		253		297		341	
34		78		122		166		210		254		298		342	
35		79		123		167		211		255		299		343	
36		80		124		168		212		256		300		344	
37		81		125		169		213		257		301		345	
38		82		126		170		214		258		302		346	
39		83		127		171		215		259		303		347	
40		84		128		172		216		260		304		348	
41		85		129		173		217		261		305		349	
42		86		130		174		218		262		306		350	
43		87		131		175		219		263		307		351	
44		88		132		176		220		264		308		352	

Fitness Planner							
	Monday	Tuesday	Wednesday	Thursday	Friday	Saturday	Sunday
Body Part							
Workout Time							
TDEE							
Exercise 1							
Reps : Sets : Rest							
Exercise 2							
Reps : Sets : Rest							
Exercise 3							
Reps : Sets : Rest							
Exercise 4							
Reps : Sets : Rest							
Exercise 5							
Reps : Sets : Rest							
Exercise 6							
Reps : Sets : Rest							
Exercise 7							
Reps : Sets : Rest							
Exercise 8							
Reps : Sets : Rest							
Exercise 9							
Reps : Sets : Rest							
Cardio Time							
Calories Burned							
Total Macros							
Total Sugars							
Meal 1							
Cal:Prot:Carb:Fat							
Meal 2							
Cal:Prot:Carb:Fat							
Meal 3							
Cal:Prot:Carb:Fat							
Meal 4							
Cal:Prot:Carb:Fat							
Meal 5							
Cal:Prot:Carb:Fat							
Meal 6							
Cal:Prot:Carb:Fat							
Cook Time							
Meal Satisfaction							
Brain Supplement							
Energy Supplement							
Micronutrient Supplement							
Notes Calculate your TDEE based on workouts and daily activity. A 20% caloric deficit is good for study days. Eat more the evening before exams and after exams.							

week 30

MCAT Date: September 9th (start log)

Daily 24-Hour Log

Date	05/15/17	05/16/17					
Days Left	117	116					
	Monday	Tuesday	Wednesday	Thursday	Friday	Saturday	Sunday
5:00 am		sleep					
6:00 am							
7:00 am							
7:30 am		Talk to parents					
8:00 am							
8:30 am							
9:00 am							
9:30 am							
10:00 am		Rest					
10:30 am		Planning					
11:00 am							
11:30 am							
12:00 pm	OBGYN						
12:30 pm							
1:00 pm							
1:30 pm							
2:00 pm							
2:30 pm							
3:00 pm							
3:30 pm							
4:00 pm	FOOD						
4:30 pm							
5:00 pm							
5:30 pm							
6:00 pm							
6:30 pm							
7:00 pm							
7:30 pm							
8:00 pm							
8:80 pm							
9:00 pm							
9:30 pm							
10:00 pm							
10:30 pm							
11:00 pm							
11:30 pm							
12:00 am							
12:30 am							
1:00 am							
2:00 am							
3:00 am							
4:00 am							
Non-MCAT Hours							
MCAT Hours	0						
Material/Score							
Material/Score							
Material/Score							
Daily Revision							
Daily CARS							
Exercise							
Nutrition							
Happiness Level							
Stress Level							
Motivation Level							
Notes							

Week Notes & Improvement Analysis							
Date							
	Monday	Tuesday	Wednesday	Thursday	Friday	Saturday	Sunday
MCAT		• AK lecture Bio-chem Video 1~22 • 3 CARS • Reread Psy section 1 Bio sec 7 • P# 8, 9					
Mental Barriers							
School/Work Efficiency							
Project 1 • Baby motion							
Project 2 • Hourly H_2O • 2 Vitamins							
Project 3 Read • Baby Book • Republic							
Project 4 • writting course							
Medical School Application							
Social Harris call parents	✓ ✓	✓					
Fitness GYM Walk Maya	O ✓						
General							

Finish content Review By 12/30/2017

Daily 24-Hour Log							
Date				10/12/2017			
Days Left				63			
	Monday	Tuesday	Wednesday	Thursday	Friday	Saturday	Sunday
5:00 am							
6:00 am							
7:00 am							
7:30 am							
8:00 am							
8:30 am							
9:00 am							
9:30 am							
10:00 am							
10:30 am							
11:00 am							
11:30 am							
12:00 pm							
12:30 pm							
1:00 pm							
1:30 pm							
2:00 pm							
2:30 pm							
3:00 pm							
3:30 pm							
4:00 pm							
4:30 pm							
5:00 pm							
5:30 pm							
6:00 pm							
6:30 pm							
7:00 pm							
7:30 pm							
8:00 pm							
8:80 pm							
9:00 pm							
9:30 pm							
10:00 pm							
10:30 pm							
11:00 pm							
11:30 pm							
12:00 am							
12:30 am							
1:00 am							
2:00 am							
3:00 am							
4:00 am							
Non-MCAT Hours							
MCAT Hours							
Material/Score							
Material/Score							
Material/Score							
Daily Revision							
Daily CARS							
Exercise							
Nutrition							
Happiness Level							
Stress Level							
Motivation Level							
Notes							

Week Notes & Improvement Analysis							
Date							
	Monday	Tuesday	Wednesday	Thursday	Friday	Saturday	Sunday
MCAT							
Mental Barriers				Early start temptation for reading useless things			
School/Work Efficiency							
Project 1				meal planning.			
Project 2				Grocery			
Project 3				chinese visa			
Project 4							
Medical School Application							
Social							
Fitness							
General							

Daily 24-Hour Log							
Date							
Days Left							
	Monday	Tuesday	Wednesday	Thursday	Friday	Saturday	Sunday
5:00 am							
6:00 am							
7:00 am							
7:30 am							
8:00 am							
8:30 am							
9:00 am							
9:30 am							
10:00 am							
10:30 am							
11:00 am							
11:30 am							
12:00 pm							
12:30 pm							
1:00 pm							
1:30 pm							
2:00 pm							
2:30 pm							
3:00 pm							
3:30 pm							
4:00 pm							
4:30 pm							
5:00 pm							
5:30 pm							
6:00 pm							
6:30 pm							
7:00 pm							
7:30 pm							
8:00 pm							
8:80 pm							
9:00 pm							
9:30 pm							
10:00 pm							
10:30 pm							
11:00 pm							
11:30 pm							
12:00 am							
12:30 am							
1:00 am							
2:00 am							
3:00 am							
4:00 am							
Non-MCAT Hours							
MCAT Hours							
Material/Score							
Material/Score							
Material/Score							
Daily Revision							
Daily CARS							
Exercise							
Nutrition							
Happiness Level							
Stress Level							
Motivation Level							
Notes							

Week Notes & Improvement Analysis							
Date							
	Monday	Tuesday	Wednesday	Thursday	Friday	Saturday	Sunday
MCAT							
Mental Barriers							
School/Work Efficiency							
Project 1							
Project 2							
Project 3							
Project 4							
Medical School Application							
Social							
Fitness							
General							

Daily 24-Hour Log							
Date							
Days Left							
	Monday	Tuesday	Wednesday	Thursday	Friday	Saturday	Sunday
5:00 am							
6:00 am							
7:00 am							
7:30 am							
8:00 am							
8:30 am							
9:00 am							
9:30 am							
10:00 am							
10:30 am							
11:00 am							
11:30 am							
12:00 pm							
12:30 pm							
1:00 pm							
1:30 pm							
2:00 pm							
2:30 pm							
3:00 pm							
3:30 pm							
4:00 pm							
4:30 pm							
5:00 pm							
5:30 pm							
6:00 pm							
6:30 pm							
7:00 pm							
7:30 pm							
8:00 pm							
8:80 pm							
9:00 pm							
9:30 pm							
10:00 pm							
10:30 pm							
11:00 pm							
11:30 pm							
12:00 am							
12:30 am							
1:00 am							
2:00 am							
3:00 am							
4:00 am							
Non-MCAT Hours							
MCAT Hours							
Material/Score							
Material/Score							
Material/Score							
Daily Revision							
Daily CARS							
Exercise							
Nutrition							
Happiness Level							
Stress Level							
Motivation Level							
Notes							

Week Notes & Improvement Analysis							
Date							
	Monday	Tuesday	Wednesday	Thursday	Friday	Saturday	Sunday
MCAT							
Mental Barriers							
School/Work Efficiency							
Project 1							
Project 2							
Project 3							
Project 4							
Medical School Application							
Social							
Fitness							
General							

Daily 24-Hour Log							
Date							
Days Left							
	Monday	Tuesday	Wednesday	Thursday	Friday	Saturday	Sunday
5:00 am							
6:00 am							
7:00 am							
7:30 am							
8:00 am							
8:30 am							
9:00 am							
9:30 am							
10:00 am							
10:30 am							
11:00 am							
11:30 am							
12:00 pm							
12:30 pm							
1:00 pm							
1:30 pm							
2:00 pm							
2:30 pm							
3:00 pm							
3:30 pm							
4:00 pm							
4:30 pm							
5:00 pm							
5:30 pm							
6:00 pm							
6:30 pm							
7:00 pm							
7:30 pm							
8:00 pm							
8:80 pm							
9:00 pm							
9:30 pm							
10:00 pm							
10:30 pm							
11:00 pm							
11:30 pm							
12:00 am							
12:30 am							
1:00 am							
2:00 am							
3:00 am							
4:00 am							
Non-MCAT Hours							
MCAT Hours							
Material/Score							
Material/Score							
Material/Score							
Daily Revision							
Daily CARS							
Exercise							
Nutrition							
Happiness Level							
Stress Level							
Motivation Level							
Notes							

Week Notes & Improvement Analysis							
Date							
	Monday	Tuesday	Wednesday	Thursday	Friday	Saturday	Sunday
MCAT							
Mental Barriers							
School/Work Efficiency							
Project 1							
Project 2							
Project 3							
Project 4							
Medical School Application							
Social							
Fitness							
General							

Daily 24-Hour Log							
Date							
Days Left							
	Monday	Tuesday	Wednesday	Thursday	Friday	Saturday	Sunday
5:00 am							
6:00 am							
7:00 am							
7:30 am							
8:00 am							
8:30 am							
9:00 am							
9:30 am							
10:00 am							
10:30 am							
11:00 am							
11:30 am							
12:00 pm							
12:30 pm							
1:00 pm							
1:30 pm							
2:00 pm							
2:30 pm							
3:00 pm							
3:30 pm							
4:00 pm							
4:30 pm							
5:00 pm							
5:30 pm							
6:00 pm							
6:30 pm							
7:00 pm							
7:30 pm							
8:00 pm							
8:80 pm							
9:00 pm							
9:30 pm							
10:00 pm							
10:30 pm							
11:00 pm							
11:30 pm							
12:00 am							
12:30 am							
1:00 am							
2:00 am							
3:00 am							
4:00 am							
Non-MCAT Hours							
MCAT Hours							
Material/Score							
Material/Score							
Material/Score							
Daily Revision							
Daily CARS							
Exercise							
Nutrition							
Happiness Level							
Stress Level							
Motivation Level							
Notes							

Week Notes & Improvement Analysis							
Date							
	Monday	Tuesday	Wednesday	Thursday	Friday	Saturday	Sunday
MCAT							
Mental Barriers							
School/Work Efficiency							
Project 1							
Project 2							
Project 3							
Project 4							
Medical School Application							
Social							
Fitness							
General							

Daily 24-Hour Log							
Date							
Days Left							
	Monday	Tuesday	Wednesday	Thursday	Friday	Saturday	Sunday
5:00 am							
6:00 am							
7:00 am							
7:30 am							
8:00 am							
8:30 am							
9:00 am							
9:30 am							
10:00 am							
10:30 am							
11:00 am							
11:30 am							
12:00 pm							
12:30 pm							
1:00 pm							
1:30 pm							
2:00 pm							
2:30 pm							
3:00 pm							
3:30 pm							
4:00 pm							
4:30 pm							
5:00 pm							
5:30 pm							
6:00 pm							
6:30 pm							
7:00 pm							
7:30 pm							
8:00 pm							
8:80 pm							
9:00 pm							
9:30 pm							
10:00 pm							
10:30 pm							
11:00 pm							
11:30 pm							
12:00 am							
12:30 am							
1:00 am							
2:00 am							
3:00 am							
4:00 am							
Non-MCAT Hours							
MCAT Hours							
Material/Score							
Material/Score							
Material/Score							
Daily Revision							
Daily CARS							
Exercise							
Nutrition							
Happiness Level							
Stress Level							
Motivation Level							
Notes							

Week Notes & Improvement Analysis							
Date							
	Monday	Tuesday	Wednesday	Thursday	Friday	Saturday	Sunday
MCAT							
Mental Barriers							
School/Work Efficiency							
Project 1							
Project 2							
Project 3							
Project 4							
Medical School Application							
Social							
Fitness							
General							

Daily 24-Hour Log							
Date							
Days Left							
	Monday	Tuesday	Wednesday	Thursday	Friday	Saturday	Sunday
5:00 am							
6:00 am							
7:00 am							
7:30 am							
8:00 am							
8:30 am							
9:00 am							
9:30 am							
10:00 am							
10:30 am							
11:00 am							
11:30 am							
12:00 pm							
12:30 pm							
1:00 pm							
1:30 pm							
2:00 pm							
2:30 pm							
3:00 pm							
3:30 pm							
4:00 pm							
4:30 pm							
5:00 pm							
5:30 pm							
6:00 pm							
6:30 pm							
7:00 pm							
7:30 pm							
8:00 pm							
8:80 pm							
9:00 pm							
9:30 pm							
10:00 pm							
10:30 pm							
11:00 pm							
11:30 pm							
12:00 am							
12:30 am							
1:00 am							
2:00 am							
3:00 am							
4:00 am							
Non-MCAT Hours							
MCAT Hours							
Material/Score							
Material/Score							
Material/Score							
Daily Revision							
Daily CARS							
Exercise							
Nutrition							
Happiness Level							
Stress Level							
Motivation Level							
Notes							

Week Notes & Improvement Analysis							
Date							
	Monday	Tuesday	Wednesday	Thursday	Friday	Saturday	Sunday
MCAT							
Mental Barriers							
School/Work Efficiency							
Project 1							
Project 2							
Project 3							
Project 4							
Medical School Application							
Social							
Fitness							
General							

Daily 24-Hour Log							
Date							
Days Left							
	Monday	Tuesday	Wednesday	Thursday	Friday	Saturday	Sunday
5:00 am							
6:00 am							
7:00 am							
7:30 am							
8:00 am							
8:30 am							
9:00 am							
9:30 am							
10:00 am							
10:30 am							
11:00 am							
11:30 am							
12:00 pm							
12:30 pm							
1:00 pm							
1:30 pm							
2:00 pm							
2:30 pm							
3:00 pm							
3:30 pm							
4:00 pm							
4:30 pm							
5:00 pm							
5:30 pm							
6:00 pm							
6:30 pm							
7:00 pm							
7:30 pm							
8:00 pm							
8:80 pm							
9:00 pm							
9:30 pm							
10:00 pm							
10:30 pm							
11:00 pm							
11:30 pm							
12:00 am							
12:30 am							
1:00 am							
2:00 am							
3:00 am							
4:00 am							
Non-MCAT Hours							
MCAT Hours							
Material/Score							
Material/Score							
Material/Score							
Daily Revision							
Daily CARS							
Exercise							
Nutrition							
Happiness Level							
Stress Level							
Motivation Level							
Notes							

Week Notes & Improvement Analysis							
Date							
	Monday	Tuesday	Wednesday	Thursday	Friday	Saturday	Sunday
MCAT							
Mental Barriers							
School/Work Efficiency							
Project 1							
Project 2							
Project 3							
Project 4							
Medical School Application							
Social							
Fitness							
General							

Daily 24-Hour Log							
Date							
Days Left							
	Monday	Tuesday	Wednesday	Thursday	Friday	Saturday	Sunday
5:00 am							
6:00 am							
7:00 am							
7:30 am							
8:00 am							
8:30 am							
9:00 am							
9:30 am							
10:00 am							
10:30 am							
11:00 am							
11:30 am							
12:00 pm							
12:30 pm							
1:00 pm							
1:30 pm							
2:00 pm							
2:30 pm							
3:00 pm							
3:30 pm							
4:00 pm							
4:30 pm							
5:00 pm							
5:30 pm							
6:00 pm							
6:30 pm							
7:00 pm							
7:30 pm							
8:00 pm							
8:80 pm							
9:00 pm							
9:30 pm							
10:00 pm							
10:30 pm							
11:00 pm							
11:30 pm							
12:00 am							
12:30 am							
1:00 am							
2:00 am							
3:00 am							
4:00 am							
Non-MCAT Hours							
MCAT Hours							
Material/Score							
Material/Score							
Material/Score							
Daily Revision							
Daily CARS							
Exercise							
Nutrition							
Happiness Level							
Stress Level							
Motivation Level							
Notes							

Week Notes & Improvement Analysis							
Date							
	Monday	Tuesday	Wednesday	Thursday	Friday	Saturday	Sunday
MCAT							
Mental Barriers							
School/Work Efficiency							
Project 1							
Project 2							
Project 3							
Project 4							
Medical School Application							
Social							
Fitness							
General							

Daily 24-Hour Log							
Date							
Days Left							
	Monday	Tuesday	Wednesday	Thursday	Friday	Saturday	Sunday
5:00 am							
6:00 am							
7:00 am							
7:30 am							
8:00 am							
8:30 am							
9:00 am							
9:30 am							
10:00 am							
10:30 am							
11:00 am							
11:30 am							
12:00 pm							
12:30 pm							
1:00 pm							
1:30 pm							
2:00 pm							
2:30 pm							
3:00 pm							
3:30 pm							
4:00 pm							
4:30 pm							
5:00 pm							
5:30 pm							
6:00 pm							
6:30 pm							
7:00 pm							
7:30 pm							
8:00 pm							
8:80 pm							
9:00 pm							
9:30 pm							
10:00 pm							
10:30 pm							
11:00 pm							
11:30 pm							
12:00 am							
12:30 am							
1:00 am							
2:00 am							
3:00 am							
4:00 am							
Non-MCAT Hours							
MCAT Hours							
Material/Score							
Material/Score							
Material/Score							
Daily Revision							
Daily CARS							
Exercise							
Nutrition							
Happiness Level							
Stress Level							
Motivation Level							
Notes							

Week Notes & Improvement Analysis							
Date							
	Monday	Tuesday	Wednesday	Thursday	Friday	Saturday	Sunday
MCAT							
Mental Barriers							
School/Work Efficiency							
Project 1							
Project 2							
Project 3							
Project 4							
Medical School Application							
Social							
Fitness							
General							

Daily 24-Hour Log							
Date							
Days Left							
	Monday	Tuesday	Wednesday	Thursday	Friday	Saturday	Sunday
5:00 am							
6:00 am							
7:00 am							
7:30 am							
8:00 am							
8:30 am							
9:00 am							
9:30 am							
10:00 am							
10:30 am							
11:00 am							
11:30 am							
12:00 pm							
12:30 pm							
1:00 pm							
1:30 pm							
2:00 pm							
2:30 pm							
3:00 pm							
3:30 pm							
4:00 pm							
4:30 pm							
5:00 pm							
5:30 pm							
6:00 pm							
6:30 pm							
7:00 pm							
7:30 pm							
8:00 pm							
8:80 pm							
9:00 pm							
9:30 pm							
10:00 pm							
10:30 pm							
11:00 pm							
11:30 pm							
12:00 am							
12:30 am							
1:00 am							
2:00 am							
3:00 am							
4:00 am							
Non-MCAT Hours							
MCAT Hours							
Material/Score							
Material/Score							
Material/Score							
Daily Revision							
Daily CARS							
Exercise							
Nutrition							
Happiness Level							
Stress Level							
Motivation Level							
Notes							

Week Notes & Improvement Analysis							
Date							
	Monday	Tuesday	Wednesday	Thursday	Friday	Saturday	Sunday
MCAT							
Mental Barriers							
School/Work Efficiency							
Project 1							
Project 2							
Project 3							
Project 4							
Medical School Application							
Social							
Fitness							
General							

Daily 24-Hour Log							
Date							
Days Left							
	Monday	Tuesday	Wednesday	Thursday	Friday	Saturday	Sunday
5:00 am							
6:00 am							
7:00 am							
7:30 am							
8:00 am							
8:30 am							
9:00 am							
9:30 am							
10:00 am							
10:30 am							
11:00 am							
11:30 am							
12:00 pm							
12:30 pm							
1:00 pm							
1:30 pm							
2:00 pm							
2:30 pm							
3:00 pm							
3:30 pm							
4:00 pm							
4:30 pm							
5:00 pm							
5:30 pm							
6:00 pm							
6:30 pm							
7:00 pm							
7:30 pm							
8:00 pm							
8:80 pm							
9:00 pm							
9:30 pm							
10:00 pm							
10:30 pm							
11:00 pm							
11:30 pm							
12:00 am							
12:30 am							
1:00 am							
2:00 am							
3:00 am							
4:00 am							
Non-MCAT Hours							
MCAT Hours							
Material/Score							
Material/Score							
Material/Score							
Daily Revision							
Daily CARS							
Exercise							
Nutrition							
Happiness Level							
Stress Level							
Motivation Level							
Notes							

Week Notes & Improvement Analysis							
Date							
	Monday	Tuesday	Wednesday	Thursday	Friday	Saturday	Sunday
MCAT							
Mental Barriers							
School/Work Efficiency							
Project 1							
Project 2							
Project 3							
Project 4							
Medical School Application							
Social							
Fitness							
General							

Daily 24-Hour Log							
Date							
Days Left							
	Monday	Tuesday	Wednesday	Thursday	Friday	Saturday	Sunday
5:00 am							
6:00 am							
7:00 am							
7:30 am							
8:00 am							
8:30 am							
9:00 am							
9:30 am							
10:00 am							
10:30 am							
11:00 am							
11:30 am							
12:00 pm							
12:30 pm							
1:00 pm							
1:30 pm							
2:00 pm							
2:30 pm							
3:00 pm							
3:30 pm							
4:00 pm							
4:30 pm							
5:00 pm							
5:30 pm							
6:00 pm							
6:30 pm							
7:00 pm							
7:30 pm							
8:00 pm							
8:80 pm							
9:00 pm							
9:30 pm							
10:00 pm							
10:30 pm							
11:00 pm							
11:30 pm							
12:00 am							
12:30 am							
1:00 am							
2:00 am							
3:00 am							
4:00 am							
Non-MCAT Hours							
MCAT Hours							
Material/Score							
Material/Score							
Material/Score							
Daily Revision							
Daily CARS							
Exercise							
Nutrition							
Happiness Level							
Stress Level							
Motivation Level							
Notes							

Week Notes & Improvement Analysis							
Date							
	Monday	Tuesday	Wednesday	Thursday	Friday	Saturday	Sunday
MCAT							
Mental Barriers							
School/Work Efficiency							
Project 1							
Project 2							
Project 3							
Project 4							
Medical School Application							
Social							
Fitness							
General							

Daily 24-Hour Log							
Date							
Days Left							
	Monday	Tuesday	Wednesday	Thursday	Friday	Saturday	Sunday
5:00 am							
6:00 am							
7:00 am							
7:30 am							
8:00 am							
8:30 am							
9:00 am							
9:30 am							
10:00 am							
10:30 am							
11:00 am							
11:30 am							
12:00 pm							
12:30 pm							
1:00 pm							
1:30 pm							
2:00 pm							
2:30 pm							
3:00 pm							
3:30 pm							
4:00 pm							
4:30 pm							
5:00 pm							
5:30 pm							
6:00 pm							
6:30 pm							
7:00 pm							
7:30 pm							
8:00 pm							
8:80 pm							
9:00 pm							
9:30 pm							
10:00 pm							
10:30 pm							
11:00 pm							
11:30 pm							
12:00 am							
12:30 am							
1:00 am							
2:00 am							
3:00 am							
4:00 am							
Non-MCAT Hours							
MCAT Hours							
Material/Score							
Material/Score							
Material/Score							
Daily Revision							
Daily CARS							
Exercise							
Nutrition							
Happiness Level							
Stress Level							
Motivation Level							
Notes							

Week Notes & Improvement Analysis							
Date							
	Monday	Tuesday	Wednesday	Thursday	Friday	Saturday	Sunday
MCAT							
Mental Barriers							
School/Work Efficiency							
Project 1							
Project 2							
Project 3							
Project 4							
Medical School Application							
Social							
Fitness							
General							

Daily 24-Hour Log							
Date							
Days Left							
	Monday	Tuesday	Wednesday	Thursday	Friday	Saturday	Sunday
5:00 am							
6:00 am							
7:00 am							
7:30 am							
8:00 am							
8:30 am							
9:00 am							
9:30 am							
10:00 am							
10:30 am							
11:00 am							
11:30 am							
12:00 pm							
12:30 pm							
1:00 pm							
1:30 pm							
2:00 pm							
2:30 pm							
3:00 pm							
3:30 pm							
4:00 pm							
4:30 pm							
5:00 pm							
5:30 pm							
6:00 pm							
6:30 pm							
7:00 pm							
7:30 pm							
8:00 pm							
8:80 pm							
9:00 pm							
9:30 pm							
10:00 pm							
10:30 pm							
11:00 pm							
11:30 pm							
12:00 am							
12:30 am							
1:00 am							
2:00 am							
3:00 am							
4:00 am							
Non-MCAT Hours							
MCAT Hours							
Material/Score							
Material/Score							
Material/Score							
Daily Revision							
Daily CARS							
Exercise							
Nutrition							
Happiness Level							
Stress Level							
Motivation Level							
Notes							

Week Notes & Improvement Analysis							
Date							
	Monday	Tuesday	Wednesday	Thursday	Friday	Saturday	Sunday
MCAT							
Mental Barriers							
School/Work Efficiency							
Project 1							
Project 2							
Project 3							
Project 4							
Medical School Application							
Social							
Fitness							
General							

Daily 24-Hour Log							
Date							
Days Left							
	Monday	Tuesday	Wednesday	Thursday	Friday	Saturday	Sunday
5:00 am							
6:00 am							
7:00 am							
7:30 am							
8:00 am							
8:30 am							
9:00 am							
9:30 am							
10:00 am							
10:30 am							
11:00 am							
11:30 am							
12:00 pm							
12:30 pm							
1:00 pm							
1:30 pm							
2:00 pm							
2:30 pm							
3:00 pm							
3:30 pm							
4:00 pm							
4:30 pm							
5:00 pm							
5:30 pm							
6:00 pm							
6:30 pm							
7:00 pm							
7:30 pm							
8:00 pm							
8:80 pm							
9:00 pm							
9:30 pm							
10:00 pm							
10:30 pm							
11:00 pm							
11:30 pm							
12:00 am							
12:30 am							
1:00 am							
2:00 am							
3:00 am							
4:00 am							
Non-MCAT Hours							
MCAT Hours							
Material/Score							
Material/Score							
Material/Score							
Daily Revision							
Daily CARS							
Exercise							
Nutrition							
Happiness Level							
Stress Level							
Motivation Level							
Notes							

Week Notes & Improvement Analysis							
Date							
	Monday	Tuesday	Wednesday	Thursday	Friday	Saturday	Sunday
MCAT							
Mental Barriers							
School/Work Efficiency							
Project 1							
Project 2							
Project 3							
Project 4							
Medical School Application							
Social							
Fitness							
General							

Daily 24-Hour Log							
Date							
Days Left							
	Monday	Tuesday	Wednesday	Thursday	Friday	Saturday	Sunday
5:00 am							
6:00 am							
7:00 am							
7:30 am							
8:00 am							
8:30 am							
9:00 am							
9:30 am							
10:00 am							
10:30 am							
11:00 am							
11:30 am							
12:00 pm							
12:30 pm							
1:00 pm							
1:30 pm							
2:00 pm							
2:30 pm							
3:00 pm							
3:30 pm							
4:00 pm							
4:30 pm							
5:00 pm							
5:30 pm							
6:00 pm							
6:30 pm							
7:00 pm							
7:30 pm							
8:00 pm							
8:80 pm							
9:00 pm							
9:30 pm							
10:00 pm							
10:30 pm							
11:00 pm							
11:30 pm							
12:00 am							
12:30 am							
1:00 am							
2:00 am							
3:00 am							
4:00 am							
Non-MCAT Hours							
MCAT Hours							
Material/Score							
Material/Score							
Material/Score							
Daily Revision							
Daily CARS							
Exercise							
Nutrition							
Happiness Level							
Stress Level							
Motivation Level							
Notes							

Week Notes & Improvement Analysis							
Date							
	Monday	Tuesday	Wednesday	Thursday	Friday	Saturday	Sunday
MCAT							
Mental Barriers							
School/Work Efficiency							
Project 1							
Project 2							
Project 3							
Project 4							
Medical School Application							
Social							
Fitness							
General							

Daily 24-Hour Log							
Date							
Days Left							
	Monday	Tuesday	Wednesday	Thursday	Friday	Saturday	Sunday
5:00 am							
6:00 am							
7:00 am							
7:30 am							
8:00 am							
8:30 am							
9:00 am							
9:30 am							
10:00 am							
10:30 am							
11:00 am							
11:30 am							
12:00 pm							
12:30 pm							
1:00 pm							
1:30 pm							
2:00 pm							
2:30 pm							
3:00 pm							
3:30 pm							
4:00 pm							
4:30 pm							
5:00 pm							
5:30 pm							
6:00 pm							
6:30 pm							
7:00 pm							
7:30 pm							
8:00 pm							
8:80 pm							
9:00 pm							
9:30 pm							
10:00 pm							
10:30 pm							
11:00 pm							
11:30 pm							
12:00 am							
12:30 am							
1:00 am							
2:00 am							
3:00 am							
4:00 am							
Non-MCAT Hours							
MCAT Hours							
Material/Score							
Material/Score							
Material/Score							
Daily Revision							
Daily CARS							
Exercise							
Nutrition							
Happiness Level							
Stress Level							
Motivation Level							
Notes							

Week Notes & Improvement Analysis							
Date							
	Monday	Tuesday	Wednesday	Thursday	Friday	Saturday	Sunday
MCAT							
Mental Barriers							
School/Work Efficiency							
Project 1							
Project 2							
Project 3							
Project 4							
Medical School Application							
Social							
Fitness							
General							

Daily 24-Hour Log							
Date							
Days Left							
	Monday	Tuesday	Wednesday	Thursday	Friday	Saturday	Sunday
5:00 am							
6:00 am							
7:00 am							
7:30 am							
8:00 am							
8:30 am							
9:00 am							
9:30 am							
10:00 am							
10:30 am							
11:00 am							
11:30 am							
12:00 pm							
12:30 pm							
1:00 pm							
1:30 pm							
2:00 pm							
2:30 pm							
3:00 pm							
3:30 pm							
4:00 pm							
4:30 pm							
5:00 pm							
5:30 pm							
6:00 pm							
6:30 pm							
7:00 pm							
7:30 pm							
8:00 pm							
8:80 pm							
9:00 pm							
9:30 pm							
10:00 pm							
10:30 pm							
11:00 pm							
11:30 pm							
12:00 am							
12:30 am							
1:00 am							
2:00 am							
3:00 am							
4:00 am							
Non-MCAT Hours							
MCAT Hours							
Material/Score							
Material/Score							
Material/Score							
Daily Revision							
Daily CARS							
Exercise							
Nutrition							
Happiness Level							
Stress Level							
Motivation Level							
Notes							

Week Notes & Improvement Analysis							
Date							
	Monday	Tuesday	Wednesday	Thursday	Friday	Saturday	Sunday
MCAT							
Mental Barriers							
School/Work Efficiency							
Project 1							
Project 2							
Project 3							
Project 4							
Medical School Application							
Social							
Fitness							
General							

Daily 24-Hour Log							
Date							
Days Left							
	Monday	Tuesday	Wednesday	Thursday	Friday	Saturday	Sunday
5:00 am							
6:00 am							
7:00 am							
7:30 am							
8:00 am							
8:30 am							
9:00 am							
9:30 am							
10:00 am							
10:30 am							
11:00 am							
11:30 am							
12:00 pm							
12:30 pm							
1:00 pm							
1:30 pm							
2:00 pm							
2:30 pm							
3:00 pm							
3:30 pm							
4:00 pm							
4:30 pm							
5:00 pm							
5:30 pm							
6:00 pm							
6:30 pm							
7:00 pm							
7:30 pm							
8:00 pm							
8:80 pm							
9:00 pm							
9:30 pm							
10:00 pm							
10:30 pm							
11:00 pm							
11:30 pm							
12:00 am							
12:30 am							
1:00 am							
2:00 am							
3:00 am							
4:00 am							
Non-MCAT Hours							
MCAT Hours							
Material/Score							
Material/Score							
Material/Score							
Daily Revision							
Daily CARS							
Exercise							
Nutrition							
Happiness Level							
Stress Level							
Motivation Level							
Notes							

Week Notes & Improvement Analysis							
Date							
	Monday	Tuesday	Wednesday	Thursday	Friday	Saturday	Sunday
MCAT							
Mental Barriers							
School/Work Efficiency							
Project 1							
Project 2							
Project 3							
Project 4							
Medical School Application							
Social							
Fitness							
General							

Daily 24-Hour Log							
Date							
Days Left							
	Monday	Tuesday	Wednesday	Thursday	Friday	Saturday	Sunday
5:00 am							
6:00 am							
7:00 am							
7:30 am							
8:00 am							
8:30 am							
9:00 am							
9:30 am							
10:00 am							
10:30 am							
11:00 am							
11:30 am							
12:00 pm							
12:30 pm							
1:00 pm							
1:30 pm							
2:00 pm							
2:30 pm							
3:00 pm							
3:30 pm							
4:00 pm							
4:30 pm							
5:00 pm							
5:30 pm							
6:00 pm							
6:30 pm							
7:00 pm							
7:30 pm							
8:00 pm							
8:80 pm							
9:00 pm							
9:30 pm							
10:00 pm							
10:30 pm							
11:00 pm							
11:30 pm							
12:00 am							
12:30 am							
1:00 am							
2:00 am							
3:00 am							
4:00 am							
Non-MCAT Hours							
MCAT Hours							
Material/Score							
Material/Score							
Material/Score							
Daily Revision							
Daily CARS							
Exercise							
Nutrition							
Happiness Level							
Stress Level							
Motivation Level							
Notes							

Week Notes & Improvement Analysis							
Date							
	Monday	Tuesday	Wednesday	Thursday	Friday	Saturday	Sunday
MCAT							
Mental Barriers							
School/Work Efficiency							
Project 1							
Project 2							
Project 3							
Project 4							
Medical School Application							
Social							
Fitness							
General							

Daily 24-Hour Log							
Date							
Days Left							
	Monday	Tuesday	Wednesday	Thursday	Friday	Saturday	Sunday
5:00 am							
6:00 am							
7:00 am							
7:30 am							
8:00 am							
8:30 am							
9:00 am							
9:30 am							
10:00 am							
10:30 am							
11:00 am							
11:30 am							
12:00 pm							
12:30 pm							
1:00 pm							
1:30 pm							
2:00 pm							
2:30 pm							
3:00 pm							
3:30 pm							
4:00 pm							
4:30 pm							
5:00 pm							
5:30 pm							
6:00 pm							
6:30 pm							
7:00 pm							
7:30 pm							
8:00 pm							
8:80 pm							
9:00 pm							
9:30 pm							
10:00 pm							
10:30 pm							
11:00 pm							
11:30 pm							
12:00 am							
12:30 am							
1:00 am							
2:00 am							
3:00 am							
4:00 am							
Non-MCAT Hours							
MCAT Hours							
Material/Score							
Material/Score							
Material/Score							
Daily Revision							
Daily CARS							
Exercise							
Nutrition							
Happiness Level							
Stress Level							
Motivation Level							
Notes							

Week Notes & Improvement Analysis							
Date							
	Monday	Tuesday	Wednesday	Thursday	Friday	Saturday	Sunday
MCAT							
Mental Barriers							
School/Work Efficiency							
Project 1							
Project 2							
Project 3							
Project 4							
Medical School Application							
Social							
Fitness							
General							

Daily 24-Hour Log							
Date							
Days Left							
	Monday	Tuesday	Wednesday	Thursday	Friday	Saturday	Sunday
5:00 am							
6:00 am							
7:00 am							
7:30 am							
8:00 am							
8:30 am							
9:00 am							
9:30 am							
10:00 am							
10:30 am							
11:00 am							
11:30 am							
12:00 pm							
12:30 pm							
1:00 pm							
1:30 pm							
2:00 pm							
2.30 pm							
3:00 pm							
3:30 pm							
4:00 pm							
4:30 pm							
5:00 pm							
5:30 pm							
6:00 pm							
6:30 pm							
7:00 pm							
7:30 pm							
8:00 pm							
8:80 pm							
9:00 pm							
9:30 pm							
10:00 pm							
10:30 pm							
11:00 pm							
11:30 pm							
12:00 am							
12:30 am							
1:00 am							
2:00 am							
3:00 am							
4:00 am							
Non-MCAT Hours							
MCAT Hours							
Material/Score							
Material/Score							
Material/Score							
Daily Revision							
Daily CARS							
Exercise							
Nutrition							
Happiness Level							
Stress Level							
Motivation Level							
Notes							

Week Notes & Improvement Analysis							
Date							
	Monday	Tuesday	Wednesday	Thursday	Friday	Saturday	Sunday
MCAT							
Mental Barriers							
School/Work Efficiency							
Project 1							
Project 2							
Project 3							
Project 4							
Medical School Application							
Social							
Fitness							
General							

Daily 24-Hour Log							
Date							
Days Left							
	Monday	Tuesday	Wednesday	Thursday	Friday	Saturday	Sunday
5:00 am							
6:00 am							
7:00 am							
7:30 am							
8:00 am							
8:30 am							
9:00 am							
9:30 am							
10:00 am							
10:30 am							
11:00 am							
11:30 am							
12:00 pm							
12:30 pm							
1:00 pm							
1:30 pm							
2:00 pm							
2:30 pm							
3:00 pm							
3:30 pm							
4:00 pm							
4:30 pm							
5:00 pm							
5:30 pm							
6:00 pm							
6:30 pm							
7:00 pm							
7:30 pm							
8:00 pm							
8:80 pm							
9:00 pm							
9:30 pm							
10:00 pm							
10:30 pm							
11:00 pm							
11:30 pm							
12:00 am							
12:30 am							
1:00 am							
2:00 am							
3:00 am							
4:00 am							
Non-MCAT Hours							
MCAT Hours							
Material/Score							
Material/Score							
Material/Score							
Daily Revision							
Daily CARS							
Exercise							
Nutrition							
Happiness Level							
Stress Level							
Motivation Level							
Notes							

Week Notes & Improvement Analysis							
Date							
	Monday	Tuesday	Wednesday	Thursday	Friday	Saturday	Sunday
MCAT							
Mental Barriers							
School/Work Efficiency							
Project 1							
Project 2							
Project 3							
Project 4							
Medical School Application							
Social							
Fitness							
General							

Daily 24-Hour Log							
Date							
Days Left							
	Monday	Tuesday	Wednesday	Thursday	Friday	Saturday	Sunday
5:00 am							
6:00 am							
7:00 am							
7:30 am							
8:00 am							
8:30 am							
9:00 am							
9:30 am							
10:00 am							
10:30 am							
11:00 am							
11:30 am							
12:00 pm							
12:30 pm							
1:00 pm							
1:30 pm							
2:00 pm							
2:30 pm							
3:00 pm							
3:30 pm							
4:00 pm							
4:30 pm							
5:00 pm							
5:30 pm							
6:00 pm							
6:30 pm							
7:00 pm							
7:30 pm							
8:00 pm							
8:80 pm							
9:00 pm							
9:30 pm							
10:00 pm							
10:30 pm							
11:00 pm							
11:30 pm							
12:00 am							
12:30 am							
1:00 am							
2:00 am							
3:00 am							
4:00 am							
Non-MCAT Hours							
MCAT Hours							
Material/Score							
Material/Score							
Material/Score							
Daily Revision							
Daily CARS							
Exercise							
Nutrition							
Happiness Level							
Stress Level							
Motivation Level							
Notes							

Week Notes & Improvement Analysis							
Date							
	Monday	Tuesday	Wednesday	Thursday	Friday	Saturday	Sunday
MCAT							
Mental Barriers							
School/Work Efficiency							
Project 1							
Project 2							
Project 3							
Project 4							
Medical School Application							
Social							
Fitness							
General							

Daily 24-Hour Log							
Date							
Days Left							
	Monday	Tuesday	Wednesday	Thursday	Friday	Saturday	Sunday
5:00 am							
6:00 am							
7:00 am							
7:30 am							
8:00 am							
8:30 am							
9:00 am							
9:30 am							
10:00 am							
10:30 am							
11:00 am							
11:30 am							
12:00 pm							
12:30 pm							
1:00 pm							
1:30 pm							
2:00 pm							
2:30 pm							
3:00 pm							
3:30 pm							
4:00 pm							
4:30 pm							
5:00 pm							
5:30 pm							
6:00 pm							
6:30 pm							
7:00 pm							
7:30 pm							
8:00 pm							
8:80 pm							
9:00 pm							
9:30 pm							
10:00 pm							
10:30 pm							
11:00 pm							
11:30 pm							
12:00 am							
12:30 am							
1:00 am							
2:00 am							
3:00 am							
4:00 am							
Non-MCAT Hours							
MCAT Hours							
Material/Score							
Material/Score							
Material/Score							
Daily Revision							
Daily CARS							
Exercise							
Nutrition							
Happiness Level							
Stress Level							
Motivation Level							
Notes							

Week Notes & Improvement Analysis							
Date							
	Monday	Tuesday	Wednesday	Thursday	Friday	Saturday	Sunday
MCAT							
Mental Barriers							
School/Work Efficiency							
Project 1							
Project 2							
Project 3							
Project 4							
Medical School Application							
Social							
Fitness							
General							

Daily 24-Hour Log							
Date							
Days Left							
	Monday	Tuesday	Wednesday	Thursday	Friday	Saturday	Sunday
5:00 am							
6:00 am							
7:00 am							
7:30 am							
8:00 am							
8:30 am							
9:00 am							
9:30 am							
10:00 am							
10:30 am							
11:00 am							
11:30 am							
12:00 pm							
12:30 pm							
1:00 pm							
1:30 pm							
2:00 pm							
2:30 pm							
3:00 pm							
3:30 pm							
4:00 pm							
4:30 pm							
5:00 pm							
5:30 pm							
6:00 pm							
6:30 pm							
7:00 pm							
7:30 pm							
8:00 pm							
8:80 pm							
9:00 pm							
9:30 pm							
10:00 pm							
10:30 pm							
11:00 pm							
11:30 pm							
12:00 am							
12:30 am							
1:00 am							
2:00 am							
3:00 am							
4:00 am							
Non-MCAT Hours							
MCAT Hours							
Material/Score							
Material/Score							
Material/Score							
Daily Revision							
Daily CARS							
Exercise							
Nutrition							
Happiness Level							
Stress Level							
Motivation Level							
Notes							

Week Notes & Improvement Analysis							
Date							
	Monday	Tuesday	Wednesday	Thursday	Friday	Saturday	Sunday
MCAT							
Mental Barriers							
School/Work Efficiency							
Project 1							
Project 2							
Project 3							
Project 4							
Medical School Application							
Social							
Fitness							
General							

Daily 24-Hour Log							
Date							
Days Left							
	Monday	Tuesday	Wednesday	Thursday	Friday	Saturday	Sunday
5:00 am							
6:00 am							
7:00 am							
7:30 am							
8:00 am							
8:30 am							
9:00 am							
9:30 am							
10:00 am							
10:30 am							
11:00 am							
11:30 am							
12:00 pm							
12:30 pm							
1:00 pm							
1:30 pm							
2:00 pm							
2:30 pm							
3:00 pm							
3:30 pm							
4:00 pm							
4:30 pm							
5:00 pm							
5:30 pm							
6:00 pm							
6:30 pm							
7:00 pm							
7:30 pm							
8:00 pm							
8:80 pm							
9:00 pm							
9:30 pm							
10:00 pm							
10:30 pm							
11:00 pm							
11:30 pm							
12:00 am							
12:30 am							
1:00 am							
2:00 am							
3:00 am							
4:00 am							
Non-MCAT Hours							
MCAT Hours							
Material/Score							
Material/Score							
Material/Score							
Daily Revision							
Daily CARS							
Exercise							
Nutrition							
Happiness Level							
Stress Level							
Motivation Level							
Notes							

Week Notes & Improvement Analysis							
Date							
	Monday	Tuesday	Wednesday	Thursday	Friday	Saturday	Sunday
MCAT							
Mental Barriers							
School/Work Efficiency							
Project 1							
Project 2							
Project 3							
Project 4							
Medical School Application							
Social							
Fitness							
General							

Daily 24-Hour Log							
Date							
Days Left							
	Monday	Tuesday	Wednesday	Thursday	Friday	Saturday	Sunday
5:00 am							
6:00 am							
7:00 am							
7:30 am							
8:00 am							
8:30 am							
9:00 am							
9:30 am							
10:00 am							
10:30 am							
11:00 am							
11:30 am							
12:00 pm							
12:30 pm							
1:00 pm							
1:30 pm							
2:00 pm							
2:30 pm							
3:00 pm							
3:30 pm							
4:00 pm							
4:30 pm							
5:00 pm							
5:30 pm							
6:00 pm							
6:30 pm							
7:00 pm							
7:30 pm							
8:00 pm							
8:80 pm							
9:00 pm							
9:30 pm							
10:00 pm							
10:30 pm							
11:00 pm							
11:30 pm							
12:00 am							
12:30 am							
1:00 am							
2:00 am							
3:00 am							
4:00 am							
Non-MCAT Hours							
MCAT Hours							
Material/Score							
Material/Score							
Material/Score							
Daily Revision							
Daily CARS							
Exercise							
Nutrition							
Happiness Level							
Stress Level							
Motivation Level							
Notes							

Week Notes & Improvement Analysis							
Date							
	Monday	Tuesday	Wednesday	Thursday	Friday	Saturday	Sunday
MCAT							
Mental Barriers							
School/Work Efficiency							
Project 1							
Project 2							
Project 3							
Project 4							
Medical School Application							
Social							
Fitness							
General							

Daily 24-Hour Log							
Date							
Days Left							
	Monday	Tuesday	Wednesday	Thursday	Friday	Saturday	Sunday
5:00 am							
6:00 am							
7:00 am							
7:30 am							
8:00 am							
8:30 am							
9:00 am							
9:30 am							
10:00 am							
10:30 am							
11:00 am							
11:30 am							
12:00 pm							
12:30 pm							
1:00 pm							
1:30 pm							
2:00 pm							
2:30 pm							
3:00 pm							
3:30 pm							
4:00 pm							
4:30 pm							
5:00 pm							
5:30 pm							
6:00 pm							
6:30 pm							
7:00 pm							
7:30 pm							
8:00 pm							
8:80 pm							
9:00 pm							
9:30 pm							
10:00 pm							
10:30 pm							
11:00 pm							
11:30 pm							
12:00 am							
12:30 am							
1:00 am							
2:00 am							
3:00 am							
4:00 am							
Non-MCAT Hours							
MCAT Hours							
Material/Score							
Material/Score							
Material/Score							
Daily Revision							
Daily CARS							
Exercise							
Nutrition							
Happiness Level							
Stress Level							
Motivation Level							
Notes							

Week Notes & Improvement Analysis							
Date							
	Monday	Tuesday	Wednesday	Thursday	Friday	Saturday	Sunday
MCAT							
Mental Barriers							
School/Work Efficiency							
Project 1							
Project 2							
Project 3							
Project 4							
Medical School Application							
Social							
Fitness							
General							

Daily 24-Hour Log							
Date							
Days Left							
	Monday	Tuesday	Wednesday	Thursday	Friday	Saturday	Sunday
5:00 am							
6:00 am							
7:00 am							
7:30 am							
8:00 am							
8:30 am							
9:00 am							
9:30 am							
10:00 am							
10:30 am							
11:00 am							
11:30 am							
12:00 pm							
12:30 pm							
1:00 pm							
1:30 pm							
2:00 pm							
2:30 pm							
3:00 pm							
3:30 pm							
4:00 pm							
4:30 pm							
5:00 pm							
5:30 pm							
6:00 pm							
6:30 pm							
7:00 pm							
7:30 pm							
8:00 pm							
8:80 pm							
9:00 pm							
9:30 pm							
10:00 pm							
10:30 pm							
11:00 pm							
11:30 pm							
12:00 am							
12:30 am							
1:00 am							
2:00 am							
3:00 am							
4:00 am							
Non-MCAT Hours							
MCAT Hours							
Material/Score							
Material/Score							
Material/Score							
Daily Revision							
Daily CARS							
Exercise							
Nutrition							
Happiness Level							
Stress Level							
Motivation Level							
Notes							

Week Notes & Improvement Analysis							
Date							
	Monday	Tuesday	Wednesday	Thursday	Friday	Saturday	Sunday
MCAT							
Mental Barriers							
School/Work Efficiency							
Project 1							
Project 2							
Project 3							
Project 4							
Medical School Application							
Social							
Fitness							
General							

Daily 24-Hour Log							
Date							
Days Left							
	Monday	Tuesday	Wednesday	Thursday	Friday	Saturday	Sunday
5:00 am							
6:00 am							
7:00 am							
7:30 am							
8:00 am							
8:30 am							
9:00 am							
9:30 am							
10:00 am							
10:30 am							
11:00 am							
11:30 am							
12:00 pm							
12:30 pm							
1:00 pm							
1:30 pm							
2:00 pm							
2:30 pm							
3:00 pm							
3:30 pm							
4:00 pm							
4:30 pm							
5:00 pm							
5:30 pm							
6:00 pm							
6:30 pm							
7:00 pm							
7:30 pm							
8:00 pm							
8:80 pm							
9:00 pm							
9:30 pm							
10:00 pm							
10:30 pm							
11:00 pm							
11:30 pm							
12:00 am							
12:30 am							
1:00 am							
2:00 am							
3:00 am							
4:00 am							
Non-MCAT Hours							
MCAT Hours							
Material/Score							
Material/Score							
Material/Score							
Daily Revision							
Daily CARS							
Exercise							
Nutrition							
Happiness Level							
Stress Level							
Motivation Level							
Notes							

Week Notes & Improvement Analysis							
Date							
	Monday	Tuesday	Wednesday	Thursday	Friday	Saturday	Sunday
MCAT							
Mental Barriers							
School/Work Efficiency							
Project 1							
Project 2							
Project 3							
Project 4							
Medical School Application							
Social							
Fitness							
General							

Daily 24-Hour Log							
Date							
Days Left							
	Monday	Tuesday	Wednesday	Thursday	Friday	Saturday	Sunday
5:00 am							
6:00 am							
7:00 am							
7:30 am							
8:00 am							
8:30 am							
9:00 am							
9:30 am							
10:00 am							
10:30 am							
11:00 am							
11:30 am							
12:00 pm							
12:30 pm							
1:00 pm							
1:30 pm							
2:00 pm							
2:30 pm							
3:00 pm							
3:30 pm							
4:00 pm							
4:30 pm							
5:00 pm							
5:30 pm							
6:00 pm							
6:30 pm							
7:00 pm							
7:30 pm							
8:00 pm							
8:80 pm							
9:00 pm							
9:30 pm							
10:00 pm							
10:30 pm							
11:00 pm							
11:30 pm							
12:00 am							
12:30 am							
1:00 am							
2:00 am							
3:00 am							
4:00 am							
Non-MCAT Hours							
MCAT Hours							
Material/Score							
Material/Score							
Material/Score							
Daily Revision							
Daily CARS							
Exercise							
Nutrition							
Happiness Level							
Stress Level							
Motivation Level							
Notes							

Week Notes & Improvement Analysis							
Date							
	Monday	Tuesday	Wednesday	Thursday	Friday	Saturday	Sunday
MCAT							
Mental Barriers							
School/Work Efficiency							
Project 1							
Project 2							
Project 3							
Project 4							
Medical School Application							
Social							
Fitness							
General							

Daily 24-Hour Log							
Date							
Days Left							
	Monday	Tuesday	Wednesday	Thursday	Friday	Saturday	Sunday
5:00 am							
6:00 am							
7:00 am							
7:30 am							
8:00 am							
8:30 am							
9:00 am							
9:30 am							
10:00 am							
10:30 am							
11:00 am							
11:30 am							
12:00 pm							
12:30 pm							
1:00 pm							
1:30 pm							
2:00 pm							
2:30 pm							
3:00 pm							
3:30 pm							
4:00 pm							
4:30 pm							
5:00 pm							
5:30 pm							
6:00 pm							
6:30 pm							
7:00 pm							
7:30 pm							
8:00 pm							
8:80 pm							
9:00 pm							
9:30 pm							
10:00 pm							
10:30 pm							
11:00 pm							
11:30 pm							
12:00 am							
12:30 am							
1:00 am							
2:00 am							
3:00 am							
4:00 am							
Non-MCAT Hours							
MCAT Hours							
Material/Score							
Material/Score							
Material/Score							
Daily Revision							
Daily CARS							
Exercise							
Nutrition							
Happiness Level							
Stress Level							
Motivation Level							
Notes							

Week Notes & Improvement Analysis							
Date							
	Monday	Tuesday	Wednesday	Thursday	Friday	Saturday	Sunday
MCAT							
Mental Barriers							
School/Work Efficiency							
Project 1							
Project 2							
Project 3							
Project 4							
Medical School Application							
Social							
Fitness							
General							

Daily 24-Hour Log							
Date							
Days Left							
	Monday	Tuesday	Wednesday	Thursday	Friday	Saturday	Sunday
5:00 am							
6:00 am							
7:00 am							
7:30 am							
8:00 am							
8:30 am							
9:00 am							
9:30 am							
10:00 am							
10:30 am							
11:00 am							
11:30 am							
12:00 pm							
12:30 pm							
1:00 pm							
1:30 pm							
2:00 pm							
2:30 pm							
3:00 pm							
3:30 pm							
4:00 pm							
4:30 pm							
5:00 pm							
5:30 pm							
6:00 pm							
6:30 pm							
7:00 pm							
7:30 pm							
8:00 pm							
8:80 pm							
9:00 pm							
9:30 pm							
10:00 pm							
10:30 pm							
11:00 pm							
11:30 pm							
12:00 am							
12:30 am							
1:00 am							
2:00 am							
3:00 am							
4:00 am							
Non-MCAT Hours							
MCAT Hours							
Material/Score							
Material/Score							
Material/Score							
Daily Revision							
Daily CARS							
Exercise							
Nutrition							
Happiness Level							
Stress Level							
Motivation Level							
Notes							

Week Notes & Improvement Analysis							
Date							
	Monday	Tuesday	Wednesday	Thursday	Friday	Saturday	Sunday
MCAT							
Mental Barriers							
School/Work Efficiency							
Project 1							
Project 2							
Project 3							
Project 4							
Medical School Application							
Social							
Fitness							
General							

Daily 24-Hour Log							
Date							
Days Left							
	Monday	Tuesday	Wednesday	Thursday	Friday	Saturday	Sunday
5:00 am							
6:00 am							
7:00 am							
7:30 am							
8:00 am							
8:30 am							
9:00 am							
9:30 am							
10:00 am							
10:30 am							
11:00 am							
11:30 am							
12:00 pm							
12:30 pm							
1:00 pm							
1:30 pm							
2:00 pm							
2:30 pm							
3:00 pm							
3:30 pm							
4:00 pm							
4:30 pm							
5:00 pm							
5:30 pm							
6:00 pm							
6:30 pm							
7:00 pm							
7:30 pm							
8:00 pm							
8:80 pm							
9:00 pm							
9:30 pm							
10:00 pm							
10:30 pm							
11:00 pm							
11:30 pm							
12:00 am							
12:30 am							
1:00 am							
2:00 am							
3:00 am							
4:00 am							
Non-MCAT Hours							
MCAT Hours							
Material/Score							
Material/Score							
Material/Score							
Daily Revision							
Daily CARS							
Exercise							
Nutrition							
Happiness Level							
Stress Level							
Motivation Level							
Notes							

Week Notes & Improvement Analysis							
Date							
	Monday	Tuesday	Wednesday	Thursday	Friday	Saturday	Sunday
MCAT							
Mental Barriers							
School/Work Efficiency							
Project 1							
Project 2							
Project 3							
Project 4							
Medical School Application							
Social							
Fitness							
General							

Daily 24-Hour Log							
Date							
Days Left							
	Monday	Tuesday	Wednesday	Thursday	Friday	Saturday	Sunday
5:00 am							
6:00 am							
7:00 am							
7:30 am							
8:00 am							
8:30 am							
9:00 am							
9:30 am							
10:00 am							
10:30 am							
11:00 am							
11:30 am							
12:00 pm							
12:30 pm							
1:00 pm							
1:30 pm							
2:00 pm							
2:30 pm							
3:00 pm							
3:30 pm							
4:00 pm							
4:30 pm							
5:00 pm							
5:30 pm							
6:00 pm							
6:30 pm							
7:00 pm							
7:30 pm							
8:00 pm							
8:80 pm							
9:00 pm							
9:30 pm							
10:00 pm							
10:30 pm							
11:00 pm							
11:30 pm							
12:00 am							
12:30 am							
1:00 am							
2:00 am							
3:00 am							
4:00 am							
Non-MCAT Hours							
MCAT Hours							
Material/Score							
Material/Score							
Material/Score							
Daily Revision							
Daily CARS							
Exercise							
Nutrition							
Happiness Level							
Stress Level							
Motivation Level							
Notes							

Week Notes & Improvement Analysis							
Date							
	Monday	Tuesday	Wednesday	Thursday	Friday	Saturday	Sunday
MCAT							
Mental Barriers							
School/Work Efficiency							
Project 1							
Project 2							
Project 3							
Project 4							
Medical School Application							
Social							
Fitness							
General							

Daily 24-Hour Log							
Date							
Days Left							
	Monday	Tuesday	Wednesday	Thursday	Friday	Saturday	Sunday
5:00 am							
6:00 am							
7:00 am							
7:30 am							
8:00 am							
8:30 am							
9:00 am							
9:30 am							
10:00 am							
10:30 am							
11:00 am							
11:30 am							
12:00 pm							
12:30 pm							
1:00 pm							
1:30 pm							
2:00 pm							
2:30 pm							
3:00 pm							
3:30 pm							
4:00 pm							
4:30 pm							
5:00 pm							
5:30 pm							
6:00 pm							
6:30 pm							
7:00 pm							
7:30 pm							
8:00 pm							
8:80 pm							
9:00 pm							
9:30 pm							
10:00 pm							
10:30 pm							
11:00 pm							
11:30 pm							
12:00 am							
12:30 am							
1:00 am							
2:00 am							
3:00 am							
4:00 am							
Non-MCAT Hours							
MCAT Hours							
Material/Score							
Material/Score							
Material/Score							
Daily Revision							
Daily CARS							
Exercise							
Nutrition							
Happiness Level							
Stress Level							
Motivation Level							
Notes							

Week Notes & Improvement Analysis							
Date							
	Monday	Tuesday	Wednesday	Thursday	Friday	Saturday	Sunday
MCAT							
Mental Barriers							
School/Work Efficiency							
Project 1							
Project 2							
Project 3							
Project 4							
Medical School Application							
Social							
Fitness							
General							

Daily 24-Hour Log							
Date							
Days Left							
	Monday	Tuesday	Wednesday	Thursday	Friday	Saturday	Sunday
5:00 am							
6:00 am							
7:00 am							
7:30 am							
8:00 am							
8:30 am							
9:00 am							
9:30 am							
10:00 am							
10:30 am							
11:00 am							
11:30 am							
12:00 pm							
12:30 pm							
1:00 pm							
1:30 pm							
2:00 pm							
2:30 pm							
3:00 pm							
3:30 pm							
4:00 pm							
4:30 pm							
5:00 pm							
5:30 pm							
6:00 pm							
6:30 pm							
7:00 pm							
7:30 pm							
8:00 pm							
8:80 pm							
9:00 pm							
9:30 pm							
10:00 pm							
10:30 pm							
11:00 pm							
11:30 pm							
12:00 am							
12:30 am							
1:00 am							
2:00 am							
3:00 am							
4:00 am							
Non-MCAT Hours							
MCAT Hours							
Material/Score							
Material/Score							
Material/Score							
Daily Revision							
Daily CARS							
Exercise							
Nutrition							
Happiness Level							
Stress Level							
Motivation Level							
Notes							

Week Notes & Improvement Analysis							
Date							
	Monday	Tuesday	Wednesday	Thursday	Friday	Saturday	Sunday
MCAT							
Mental Barriers							
School/Work Efficiency							
Project 1							
Project 2							
Project 3							
Project 4							
Medical School Application							
Social							
Fitness							
General							

Daily 24-Hour Log							
Date							
Days Left							
	Monday	Tuesday	Wednesday	Thursday	Friday	Saturday	Sunday
5:00 am							
6:00 am							
7:00 am							
7:30 am							
8:00 am							
8:30 am							
9:00 am							
9:30 am							
10:00 am							
10:30 am							
11:00 am							
11:30 am							
12:00 pm							
12:30 pm							
1:00 pm							
1:30 pm							
2:00 pm							
2:30 pm							
3:00 pm							
3:30 pm							
4:00 pm							
4:30 pm							
5:00 pm							
5:30 pm							
6:00 pm							
6:30 pm							
7:00 pm							
7:30 pm							
8:00 pm							
8:80 pm							
9:00 pm							
9:30 pm							
10:00 pm							
10:30 pm							
11:00 pm							
11:30 pm							
12:00 am							
12:30 am							
1:00 am							
2:00 am							
3:00 am							
4:00 am							
Non-MCAT Hours							
MCAT Hours							
Material/Score							
Material/Score							
Material/Score							
Daily Revision							
Daily CARS							
Exercise							
Nutrition							
Happiness Level							
Stress Level							
Motivation Level							
Notes							

Week Notes & Improvement Analysis							
Date							
	Monday	Tuesday	Wednesday	Thursday	Friday	Saturday	Sunday
MCAT							
Mental Barriers							
School/Work Efficiency							
Project 1							
Project 2							
Project 3							
Project 4							
Medical School Application							
Social							
Fitness							
General							

Daily 24-Hour Log							
Date							
Days Left							
	Monday	Tuesday	Wednesday	Thursday	Friday	Saturday	Sunday
5:00 am							
6:00 am							
7:00 am							
7:30 am							
8:00 am							
8:30 am							
9:00 am							
9:30 am							
10:00 am							
10:30 am							
11:00 am							
11:30 am							
12:00 pm							
12:30 pm							
1:00 pm							
1:30 pm							
2:00 pm							
2:30 pm							
3:00 pm							
3:30 pm							
4:00 pm							
4:30 pm							
5:00 pm							
5:30 pm							
6:00 pm							
6:30 pm							
7:00 pm							
7:30 pm							
8:00 pm							
8:80 pm							
9:00 pm							
9:30 pm							
10:00 pm							
10:30 pm							
11:00 pm							
11:30 pm							
12:00 am							
12:30 am							
1:00 am							
2:00 am							
3:00 am							
4:00 am							
Non-MCAT Hours							
MCAT Hours							
Material/Score							
Material/Score							
Material/Score							
Daily Revision							
Daily CARS							
Exercise							
Nutrition							
Happiness Level							
Stress Level							
Motivation Level							
Notes							

Week Notes & Improvement Analysis							
Date							
	Monday	Tuesday	Wednesday	Thursday	Friday	Saturday	Sunday
MCAT							
Mental Barriers							
School/Work Efficiency							
Project 1							
Project 2							
Project 3							
Project 4							
Medical School Application							
Social							
Fitness							
General							

Daily 24-Hour Log							
Date							
Days Left							
	Monday	Tuesday	Wednesday	Thursday	Friday	Saturday	Sunday
5:00 am							
6:00 am							
7:00 am							
7:30 am							
8:00 am							
8:30 am							
9:00 am							
9:30 am							
10:00 am							
10:30 am							
11:00 am							
11:30 am							
12:00 pm							
12:30 pm							
1:00 pm							
1:30 pm							
2:00 pm							
2:30 pm							
3:00 pm							
3:30 pm							
4:00 pm							
4:30 pm							
5:00 pm							
5:30 pm							
6:00 pm							
6:30 pm							
7:00 pm							
7:30 pm							
8:00 pm							
8:80 pm							
9:00 pm							
9:30 pm							
10:00 pm							
10:30 pm							
11:00 pm							
11:30 pm							
12:00 am							
12:30 am							
1:00 am							
2:00 am							
3:00 am							
4:00 am							
Non-MCAT Hours							
MCAT Hours							
Material/Score							
Material/Score							
Material/Score							
Daily Revision							
Daily CARS							
Exercise							
Nutrition							
Happiness Level							
Stress Level							
Motivation Level							
Notes							

Week Notes & Improvement Analysis							
Date							
	Monday	Tuesday	Wednesday	Thursday	Friday	Saturday	Sunday
MCAT							
Mental Barriers							
School/Work Efficiency							
Project 1							
Project 2							
Project 3							
Project 4							
Medical School Application							
Social							
Fitness							
General							

Daily 24-Hour Log							
Date							
Days Left							
	Monday	Tuesday	Wednesday	Thursday	Friday	Saturday	Sunday
5:00 am							
6:00 am							
7:00 am							
7:30 am							
8:00 am							
8:30 am							
9:00 am							
9:30 am							
10:00 am							
10:30 am							
11:00 am							
11:30 am							
12:00 pm							
12:30 pm							
1:00 pm							
1:30 pm							
2:00 pm							
2:30 pm							
3:00 pm							
3:30 pm							
4:00 pm							
4:30 pm							
5:00 pm							
5:30 pm							
6:00 pm							
6:30 pm							
7:00 pm							
7:30 pm							
8:00 pm							
8:80 pm							
9:00 pm							
9:30 pm							
10:00 pm							
10:30 pm							
11:00 pm							
11:30 pm							
12:00 am							
12:30 am							
1:00 am							
2:00 am							
3:00 am							
4:00 am							
Non-MCAT Hours							
MCAT Hours							
Material/Score							
Material/Score							
Material/Score							
Daily Revision							
Daily CARS							
Exercise							
Nutrition							
Happiness Level							
Stress Level							
Motivation Level							
Notes							

Week Notes & Improvement Analysis							
Date							
	Monday	Tuesday	Wednesday	Thursday	Friday	Saturday	Sunday
MCAT							
Mental Barriers							
School/Work Efficiency							
Project 1							
Project 2							
Project 3							
Project 4							
Medical School Application							
Social							
Fitness							
General							

Daily 24-Hour Log							
Date							
Days Left							
	Monday	Tuesday	Wednesday	Thursday	Friday	Saturday	Sunday
5:00 am							
6:00 am							
7:00 am							
7:30 am							
8:00 am							
8:30 am							
9:00 am							
9:30 am							
10:00 am							
10:30 am							
11:00 am							
11:30 am							
12:00 pm							
12:30 pm							
1:00 pm							
1:30 pm							
2:00 pm							
2:30 pm							
3:00 pm							
3:30 pm							
4:00 pm							
4:30 pm							
5:00 pm							
5:30 pm							
6:00 pm							
6:30 pm							
7:00 pm							
7:30 pm							
8:00 pm							
8:80 pm							
9:00 pm							
9:30 pm							
10:00 pm							
10:30 pm							
11:00 pm							
11:30 pm							
12:00 am							
12:30 am							
1:00 am							
2:00 am							
3:00 am							
4:00 am							
Non-MCAT Hours							
MCAT Hours							
Material/Score							
Material/Score							
Material/Score							
Daily Revision							
Daily CARS							
Exercise							
Nutrition							
Happiness Level							
Stress Level							
Motivation Level							
Notes							

Week Notes & Improvement Analysis							
Date							
	Monday	Tuesday	Wednesday	Thursday	Friday	Saturday	Sunday
MCAT							
Mental Barriers							
School/Work Efficiency							
Project 1							
Project 2							
Project 3							
Project 4							
Medical School Application							
Social							
Fitness							
General							

Daily 24-Hour Log							
Date							
Days Left							
	Monday	Tuesday	Wednesday	Thursday	Friday	Saturday	Sunday
5:00 am							
6:00 am							
7:00 am							
7:30 am							
8:00 am							
8:30 am							
9:00 am							
9:30 am							
10:00 am							
10:30 am							
11:00 am							
11:30 am							
12:00 pm							
12:30 pm							
1:00 pm							
1:30 pm							
2:00 pm							
2:30 pm							
3:00 pm							
3:30 pm							
4:00 pm							
4:30 pm							
5:00 pm							
5:30 pm							
6:00 pm							
6:30 pm							
7:00 pm							
7:30 pm							
8:00 pm							
8:80 pm							
9:00 pm							
9:30 pm							
10:00 pm							
10:30 pm							
11:00 pm							
11:30 pm							
12:00 am							
12:30 am							
1:00 am							
2:00 am							
3:00 am							
4:00 am							
Non-MCAT Hours							
MCAT Hours							
Material/Score							
Material/Score							
Material/Score							
Daily Revision							
Daily CARS							
Exercise							
Nutrition							
Happiness Level							
Stress Level							
Motivation Level							
Notes							

Week Notes & Improvement Analysis							
Date							
	Monday	Tuesday	Wednesday	Thursday	Friday	Saturday	Sunday
MCAT							
Mental Barriers							
School/Work Efficiency							
Project 1							
Project 2							
Project 3							
Project 4							
Medical School Application							
Social							
Fitness							
General							

Daily 24-Hour Log							
Date							
Days Left							
	Monday	Tuesday	Wednesday	Thursday	Friday	Saturday	Sunday
5:00 am							
6:00 am							
7:00 am							
7:30 am							
8:00 am							
8:30 am							
9:00 am							
9:30 am							
10:00 am							
10:30 am							
11:00 am							
11:30 am							
12:00 pm							
12:30 pm							
1:00 pm							
1:30 pm							
2:00 pm							
2:30 pm							
3:00 pm							
3:30 pm							
4:00 pm							
4:30 pm							
5:00 pm							
5:30 pm							
6:00 pm							
6:30 pm							
7:00 pm							
7:30 pm							
8:00 pm							
8:80 pm							
9:00 pm							
9:30 pm							
10:00 pm							
10:30 pm							
11:00 pm							
11:30 pm							
12:00 am							
12:30 am							
1:00 am							
2:00 am							
3:00 am							
4:00 am							
Non-MCAT Hours							
MCAT Hours							
Material/Score							
Material/Score							
Material/Score							
Daily Revision							
Daily CARS							
Exercise							
Nutrition							
Happiness Level							
Stress Level							
Motivation Level							
Notes							

Week Notes & Improvement Analysis							
Date							
	Monday	Tuesday	Wednesday	Thursday	Friday	Saturday	Sunday
MCAT							
Mental Barriers							
School/Work Efficiency							
Project 1							
Project 2							
Project 3							
Project 4							
Medical School Application							
Social							
Fitness							
General							

Daily 24-Hour Log							
Date							
Days Left							
	Monday	Tuesday	Wednesday	Thursday	Friday	Saturday	Sunday
5:00 am							
6:00 am							
7:00 am							
7:30 am							
8:00 am							
8:30 am							
9:00 am							
9:30 am							
10:00 am							
10:30 am							
11:00 am							
11:30 am							
12:00 pm							
12:30 pm							
1:00 pm							
1:30 pm							
2:00 pm							
2:30 pm							
3:00 pm							
3:30 pm							
4:00 pm							
4:30 pm							
5:00 pm							
5:30 pm							
6:00 pm							
6:30 pm							
7:00 pm							
7:30 pm							
8:00 pm							
8:80 pm							
9:00 pm							
9:30 pm							
10:00 pm							
10:30 pm							
11:00 pm							
11:30 pm							
12:00 am							
12:30 am							
1:00 am							
2:00 am							
3:00 am							
4:00 am							
Non-MCAT Hours							
MCAT Hours							
Material/Score							
Material/Score							
Material/Score							
Daily Revision							
Daily CARS							
Exercise							
Nutrition							
Happiness Level							
Stress Level							
Motivation Level							
Notes							

Week Notes & Improvement Analysis							
Date							
	Monday	Tuesday	Wednesday	Thursday	Friday	Saturday	Sunday
MCAT							
Mental Barriers							
School/Work Efficiency							
Project 1							
Project 2							
Project 3							
Project 4							
Medical School Application							
Social							
Fitness							
General							

Daily 24-Hour Log							
Date							
Days Left							
	Monday	Tuesday	Wednesday	Thursday	Friday	Saturday	Sunday
5:00 am							
6:00 am							
7:00 am							
7:30 am							
8:00 am							
8:30 am							
9:00 am							
9:30 am							
10:00 am							
10:30 am							
11:00 am							
11:30 am							
12:00 pm							
12:30 pm							
1:00 pm							
1:30 pm							
2:00 pm							
2:30 pm							
3:00 pm							
3:30 pm							
4:00 pm							
4:30 pm							
5:00 pm							
5:30 pm							
6:00 pm							
6:30 pm							
7:00 pm							
7:30 pm							
8:00 pm							
8:80 pm							
9:00 pm							
9:30 pm							
10:00 pm							
10:30 pm							
11:00 pm							
11:30 pm							
12:00 am							
12:30 am							
1:00 am							
2:00 am							
3:00 am							
4:00 am							
Non-MCAT Hours							
MCAT Hours							
Material/Score							
Material/Score							
Material/Score							
Daily Revision							
Daily CARS							
Exercise							
Nutrition							
Happiness Level							
Stress Level							
Motivation Level							
Notes							

Week Notes & Improvement Analysis							
Date							
	Monday	Tuesday	Wednesday	Thursday	Friday	Saturday	Sunday
MCAT							
Mental Barriers							
School/Work Efficiency							
Project 1							
Project 2							
Project 3							
Project 4							
Medical School Application							
Social							
Fitness							
General							

Daily 24-Hour Log							
Date							
Days Left							
	Monday	Tuesday	Wednesday	Thursday	Friday	Saturday	Sunday
5:00 am							
6:00 am							
7:00 am							
7:30 am							
8:00 am							
8:30 am							
9:00 am							
9:30 am							
10:00 am							
10:30 am							
11:00 am							
11:30 am							
12:00 pm							
12:30 pm							
1:00 pm							
1:30 pm							
2:00 pm							
2:30 pm							
3:00 pm							
3:30 pm							
4:00 pm							
4:30 pm							
5:00 pm							
5:30 pm							
6:00 pm							
6:30 pm							
7:00 pm							
7:30 pm							
8:00 pm							
8:80 pm							
9:00 pm							
9:30 pm							
10:00 pm							
10:30 pm							
11:00 pm							
11:30 pm							
12:00 am							
12:30 am							
1:00 am							
2:00 am							
3:00 am							
4:00 am							
Non-MCAT Hours							
MCAT Hours							
Material/Score							
Material/Score							
Material/Score							
Daily Revision							
Daily CARS							
Exercise							
Nutrition							
Happiness Level							
Stress Level							
Motivation Level							
Notes							

Week Notes & Improvement Analysis							
Date							
	Monday	Tuesday	Wednesday	Thursday	Friday	Saturday	Sunday
MCAT							
Mental Barriers							
School/Work Efficiency							
Project 1							
Project 2							
Project 3							
Project 4							
Medical School Application							
Social							
Fitness							
General							

Daily 24-Hour Log							
Date							
Days Left							
	Monday	Tuesday	Wednesday	Thursday	Friday	Saturday	Sunday
5:00 am							
6:00 am							
7:00 am							
7:30 am							
8:00 am							
8:30 am							
9:00 am							
9:30 am							
10:00 am							
10:30 am							
11:00 am							
11:30 am							
12:00 pm							
12:30 pm							
1:00 pm							
1:30 pm							
2:00 pm							
2:30 pm							
3:00 pm							
3:30 pm							
4:00 pm							
4:30 pm							
5:00 pm							
5:30 pm							
6:00 pm							
6:30 pm							
7:00 pm							
7:30 pm							
8:00 pm							
8:80 pm							
9:00 pm							
9:30 pm							
10:00 pm							
10:30 pm							
11:00 pm							
11:30 pm							
12:00 am							
12:30 am							
1:00 am							
2:00 am							
3:00 am							
4:00 am							
Non-MCAT Hours							
MCAT Hours							
Material/Score							
Material/Score							
Material/Score							
Daily Revision							
Daily CARS							
Exercise							
Nutrition							
Happiness Level							
Stress Level							
Motivation Level							
Notes							

Week Notes & Improvement Analysis							
Date							
	Monday	Tuesday	Wednesday	Thursday	Friday	Saturday	Sunday
MCAT							
Mental Barriers							
School/Work Efficiency							
Project 1							
Project 2							
Project 3							
Project 4							
Medical School Application							
Social							
Fitness							
General							

Daily 24-Hour Log							
Date							
Days Left							
	Monday	Tuesday	Wednesday	Thursday	Friday	Saturday	Sunday
5:00 am							
6:00 am							
7:00 am							
7:30 am							
8:00 am							
8:30 am							
9:00 am							
9:30 am							
10:00 am							
10:30 am							
11:00 am							
11:30 am							
12:00 pm							
12:30 pm							
1:00 pm							
1:30 pm							
2:00 pm							
2:30 pm							
3:00 pm							
3:30 pm							
4:00 pm							
4:30 pm							
5:00 pm							
5:30 pm							
6:00 pm							
6:30 pm							
7:00 pm							
7:30 pm							
8:00 pm							
8:80 pm							
9:00 pm							
9:30 pm							
10:00 pm							
10:30 pm							
11:00 pm							
11:30 pm							
12:00 am							
12:30 am							
1:00 am							
2:00 am							
3:00 am							
4:00 am							
Non-MCAT Hours							
MCAT Hours							
Material/Score							
Material/Score							
Material/Score							
Daily Revision							
Daily CARS							
Exercise							
Nutrition							
Happiness Level							
Stress Level							
Motivation Level							
Notes							

Week Notes & Improvement Analysis							
Date							
	Monday	Tuesday	Wednesday	Thursday	Friday	Saturday	Sunday
MCAT							
Mental Barriers							
School/Work Efficiency							
Project 1							
Project 2							
Project 3							
Project 4							
Medical School Application							
Social							
Fitness							
General							

Daily 24-Hour Log							
Date							
Days Left							
	Monday	Tuesday	Wednesday	Thursday	Friday	Saturday	Sunday
5:00 am							
6:00 am							
7:00 am							
7:30 am							
8:00 am							
8:30 am							
9:00 am							
9:30 am							
10:00 am							
10:30 am							
11:00 am							
11:30 am							
12:00 pm							
12:30 pm							
1:00 pm							
1:30 pm							
2:00 pm							
2:30 pm							
3:00 pm							
3:30 pm							
4:00 pm							
4:30 pm							
5:00 pm							
5:30 pm							
6:00 pm							
6:30 pm							
7:00 pm							
7:30 pm							
8:00 pm							
8:80 pm							
9:00 pm							
9:30 pm							
10:00 pm							
10:30 pm							
11:00 pm							
11:30 pm							
12:00 am							
12:30 am							
1:00 am							
2:00 am							
3:00 am							
4:00 am							
Non-MCAT Hours							
MCAT Hours							
Material/Score							
Material/Score							
Material/Score							
Daily Revision							
Daily CARS							
Exercise							
Nutrition							
Happiness Level							
Stress Level							
Motivation Level							
Notes							

Week Notes & Improvement Analysis							
Date							
	Monday	Tuesday	Wednesday	Thursday	Friday	Saturday	Sunday
MCAT							
Mental Barriers							
School/Work Efficiency							
Project 1							
Project 2							
Project 3							
Project 4							
Medical School Application							
Social							
Fitness							
General							

Daily 24-Hour Log							
Date							
Days Left							
	Monday	Tuesday	Wednesday	Thursday	Friday	Saturday	Sunday
5:00 am							
6:00 am							
7:00 am							
7:30 am							
8:00 am							
8:30 am							
9:00 am							
9:30 am							
10:00 am							
10:30 am							
11:00 am							
11:30 am							
12:00 pm							
12:30 pm							
1:00 pm							
1:30 pm							
2:00 pm							
2:30 pm							
3:00 pm							
3:30 pm							
4:00 pm							
4:30 pm							
5:00 pm							
5:30 pm							
6:00 pm							
6:30 pm							
7:00 pm							
7:30 pm							
8:00 pm							
8:80 pm							
9:00 pm							
9:30 pm							
10:00 pm							
10:30 pm							
11:00 pm							
11:30 pm							
12:00 am							
12:30 am							
1:00 am							
2:00 am							
3:00 am							
4:00 am							
Non-MCAT Hours							
MCAT Hours							
Material/Score							
Material/Score							
Material/Score							
Daily Revision							
Daily CARS							
Exercise							
Nutrition							
Happiness Level							
Stress Level							
Motivation Level							
Notes							

Week Notes & Improvement Analysis							
Date							
	Monday	Tuesday	Wednesday	Thursday	Friday	Saturday	Sunday
MCAT							
Mental Barriers							
School/Work Efficiency							
Project 1							
Project 2							
Project 3							
Project 4							
Medical School Application							
Social							
Fitness							
General							

General Material Tracker								
	Material Title	MCAT Subject	Time Spent	# of MCQs or # of Chapters	Times Reviewed	Cost	Note Style	Scores
1								
2								
3								
4								
5								
6								
7								
8								
9								
10								
11								
12								
13								
14								
15								
16								
17								
18								
19								
20								
21								
22								
23								
24								
25								
26								
27								
28								
29								
30								
31								
32								
33								
34								
35								
36								
37								
38								
39								
40								
41								
42								
43								
44								
56								
Tips	Please use what you feel is appropriate. Stick to printed materials for content review as research has shown content is more difficult to retain through online review. Do not skip around materials as it may cause confusion or decrease study speed. You can learn new content without taking a class on it. Stay away from text books until you absolutely need it.	Don't follow generic plans. Do more content review for YOUR weak areas. They are unique and different from everyone else. If you are taking a class for the subject, wait until near the end or prior to starting the class to study the material.	Aim to increase reading speed over time. Take notes directly in book or WHILE reading (don't look down) to increase spread. Use a 10 minute timer with 30 second breaks to work on increasing speed. Aim for 1 minute max per question. Review content questions answers right after each question. Research any lacking content after you finish your total review rather than in between your practice. Use earplugs and study in a distraction-free area. Use website blockers and turn your phone off.	Aim for 1,000-2,000 questions per subject. Please contact us if you feel you cannot find enough questions for this. Aim for 500-700 questions in research techniques and analysis. Actively cross out what you KNOW or what is useless in books or questions to condense material that still needs to be learned.	Review at most 3 times. Review right after completion for highest retention. Never review what you already know. Understand what you don't know through youtube or online review	Buy FLs first to fit your budget before buying content	-Concept maps, draw it out!, avoid wasting time on "perfect" notes, rewrite what you don't know, Do not take notes on what you already know	Aim for 85% correct on questions by end of prep. Aim for max 0-1 wrong per passage.Students usually start at 50-70% correct and reach 85% correct at the end of content review.

Material Title	MCAT Subject	Time Spent	# of MCQs or # of Chapters	Times Reviewed	Cost	Note Style	Scores

Note Topic	General Notes
1	
2	
3	
4	
5	
6	
7	
8	
9	
10	
11	
12	
13	
14	
15	
16	
17	
18	
19	
20	
21	
22	
23	
24	
25	
26	
27	
28	
29	
30	
31	
32	
33	
34	
35	
36	
37	
38	
39	
40	
41	
42	
43	
44	
45	
46	
47	
48	
49	
50	
51	
52	
53	
54	
56	
57	
58	
59	
60	
61	
62	
63	
64	

Material Title	MCAT Subject	Time Spent	# of MCQs or # of Chapters	Times Reviewed	Cost	Note Style	Scores

Note Topic	General Notes
1	
2	
3	
4	
5	
6	
7	
8	
9	
10	
11	
12	
13	
14	
15	
16	
17	
18	
19	
20	
21	
22	
23	
24	
25	
26	
27	
28	
29	
30	
31	
32	
33	
34	
35	
36	
37	
38	
39	
40	
41	
42	
43	
44	
45	
46	
47	
48	
49	
50	
51	
52	
53	
54	
56	
57	
58	
59	
60	
61	
62	
63	
64	

Material Title	MCAT Subject	Time Spent	# of MCQs or # of Chapters	Times Reviewed	Cost	Note Style	Scores

Note Topic	General Notes
1	
2	
3	
4	
5	
6	
7	
8	
9	
10	
11	
12	
13	
14	
15	
16	
17	
18	
19	
20	
21	
22	
23	
24	
25	
26	
27	
28	
29	
30	
31	
32	
33	
34	
35	
36	
37	
38	
39	
40	
41	
42	
43	
44	
45	
46	
47	
48	
49	
50	
51	
52	
53	
54	
56	
57	
58	
59	
60	
61	
62	
63	
64	

Material Title	MCAT Subject	Time Spent	# of MCQs or # of Chapters	Times Reviewed	Cost	Note Style	Scores

Note Topic	General Notes
1	
2	
3	
4	
5	
6	
7	
8	
9	
10	
11	
12	
13	
14	
15	
16	
17	
18	
19	
20	
21	
22	
23	
24	
25	
26	
27	
28	
29	
30	
31	
32	
33	
34	
35	
36	
37	
38	
39	
40	
41	
42	
43	
44	
45	
46	
47	
48	
49	
50	
51	
52	
53	
54	
56	
57	
58	
59	
60	
61	
62	
63	
64	

Material Title	MCAT Subject	Time Spent	# of MCQs or # of Chapters	Times Reviewed	Cost	Note Style	Scores

Note Topic	General Notes
1	
2	
3	
4	
5	
6	
7	
8	
9	
10	
11	
12	
13	
14	
15	
16	
17	
18	
19	
20	
21	
22	
23	
24	
25	
26	
27	
28	
29	
30	
31	
32	
33	
34	
35	
36	
37	
38	
39	
40	
41	
42	
43	
44	
45	
46	
47	
48	
49	
50	
51	
52	
53	
54	
56	
57	
58	
59	
60	
61	
62	
63	
64	

Material Title	MCAT Subject	Time Spent	# of MCQs or # of Chapters	Times Reviewed	Cost	Note Style	Scores

Note Topic	General Notes
1	
2	
3	
4	
5	
6	
7	
8	
9	
10	
11	
12	
13	
14	
15	
16	
17	
18	
19	
20	
21	
22	
23	
24	
25	
26	
27	
28	
29	
30	
31	
32	
33	
34	
35	
36	
37	
38	
39	
40	
41	
42	
43	
44	
45	
46	
47	
48	
49	
50	
51	
52	
53	
54	
56	
57	
58	
59	
60	
61	
62	
63	
64	

Material Title	MCAT Subject	Time Spent	# of MCQs or # of Chapters	Times Reviewed	Cost	Note Style	Scores

Note Topic	General Notes
1	
2	
3	
4	
5	
6	
7	
8	
9	
10	
11	
12	
13	
14	
15	
16	
17	
18	
19	
20	
21	
22	
23	
24	
25	
26	
27	
28	
29	
30	
31	
32	
33	
34	
35	
36	
37	
38	
39	
40	
41	
42	
43	
44	
45	
46	
47	
48	
49	
50	
51	
52	
53	
54	
56	
57	
58	
59	
60	
61	
62	
63	
64	

Material Title	MCAT Subject	Time Spent	# of MCQs or # of Chapters	Times Reviewed	Cost	Note Style	Scores

Note Topic	General Notes
1	
2	
3	
4	
5	
6	
7	
8	
9	
10	
11	
12	
13	
14	
15	
16	
17	
18	
19	
20	
21	
22	
23	
24	
25	
26	
27	
28	
29	
30	
31	
32	
33	
34	
35	
36	
37	
38	
39	
40	
41	
42	
43	
44	
45	
46	
47	
48	
49	
50	
51	
52	
53	
54	
56	
57	
58	
59	
60	
61	
62	
63	
64	

Material Title	MCAT Subject	Time Spent	# of MCQs or # of Chapters	Times Reviewed	Cost	Note Style	Scores

Note Topic	General Notes
1	
2	
3	
4	
5	
6	
7	
8	
9	
10	
11	
12	
13	
14	
15	
16	
17	
18	
19	
20	
21	
22	
23	
24	
25	
26	
27	
28	
29	
30	
31	
32	
33	
34	
35	
36	
37	
38	
39	
40	
41	
42	
43	
44	
45	
46	
47	
48	
49	
50	
51	
52	
53	
54	
56	
57	
58	
59	
60	
61	
62	
63	
64	

Material Title	MCAT Subject	Time Spent	# of MCQs or # of Chapters	Times Reviewed	Cost	Note Style	Scores

Note Topic	General Notes
1	
2	
3	
4	
5	
6	
7	
8	
9	
10	
11	
12	
13	
14	
15	
16	
17	
18	
19	
20	
21	
22	
23	
24	
25	
26	
27	
28	
29	
30	
31	
32	
33	
34	
35	
36	
37	
38	
39	
40	
41	
42	
43	
44	
45	
46	
47	
48	
49	
50	
51	
52	
53	
54	
56	
57	
58	
59	
60	
61	
62	
63	
64	

Material Title	MCAT Subject	Time Spent	# of MCQs or # of Chapters	Times Reviewed	Cost	Note Style	Scores

Note Topic	General Notes
1	
2	
3	
4	
5	
6	
7	
8	
9	
10	
11	
12	
13	
14	
15	
16	
17	
18	
19	
20	
21	
22	
23	
24	
25	
26	
27	
28	
29	
30	
31	
32	
33	
34	
35	
36	
37	
38	
39	
40	
41	
42	
43	
44	
45	
46	
47	
48	
49	
50	
51	
52	
53	
54	
56	
57	
58	
59	
60	
61	
62	
63	
64	

Material Title	MCAT Subject	Time Spent	# of MCQs or # of Chapters	Times Reviewed	Cost	Note Style	Scores

Note Topic	General Notes
1	
2	
3	
4	
5	
6	
7	
8	
9	
10	
11	
12	
13	
14	
15	
16	
17	
18	
19	
20	
21	
22	
23	
24	
25	
26	
27	
28	
29	
30	
31	
32	
33	
34	
35	
36	
37	
38	
39	
40	
41	
42	
43	
44	
45	
46	
47	
48	
49	
50	
51	
52	
53	
54	
56	
57	
58	
59	
60	
61	
62	
63	
64	

Material Title	MCAT Subject	Time Spent	# of MCQs or # of Chapters	Times Reviewed	Cost	Note Style	Scores

Note Topic	General Notes
1	
2	
3	
4	
5	
6	
7	
8	
9	
10	
11	
12	
13	
14	
15	
16	
17	
18	
19	
20	
21	
22	
23	
24	
25	
26	
27	
28	
29	
30	
31	
32	
33	
34	
35	
36	
37	
38	
39	
40	
41	
42	
43	
44	
45	
46	
47	
48	
49	
50	
51	
52	
53	
54	
56	
57	
58	
59	
60	
61	
62	
63	
64	

Material Title	MCAT Subject	Time Spent	# of MCQs or # of Chapters	Times Reviewed	Cost	Note Style	Scores

Note Topic	**General Notes**
1	
2	
3	
4	
5	
6	
7	
8	
9	
10	
11	
12	
13	
14	
15	
16	
17	
18	
19	
20	
21	
22	
23	
24	
25	
26	
27	
28	
29	
30	
31	
32	
33	
34	
35	
36	
37	
38	
39	
40	
41	
42	
43	
44	
45	
46	
47	
48	
49	
50	
51	
52	
53	
54	
56	
57	
58	
59	
60	
61	
62	
63	
64	

Material Title	MCAT Subject	Time Spent	# of MCQs or # of Chapters	Times Reviewed	Cost	Note Style	Scores

Note Topic	General Notes
1	
2	
3	
4	
5	
6	
7	
8	
9	
10	
11	
12	
13	
14	
15	
16	
17	
18	
19	
20	
21	
22	
23	
24	
25	
26	
27	
28	
29	
30	
31	
32	
33	
34	
35	
36	
37	
38	
39	
40	
41	
42	
43	
44	
45	
46	
47	
48	
49	
50	
51	
52	
53	
54	
56	
57	
58	
59	
60	
61	
62	
63	
64	

Material Title	MCAT Subject	Time Spent	# of MCQs or # of Chapters	Times Reviewed	Cost	Note Style	Scores

Note Topic	General Notes
1	
2	
3	
4	
5	
6	
7	
8	
9	
10	
11	
12	
13	
14	
15	
16	
17	
18	
19	
20	
21	
22	
23	
24	
25	
26	
27	
28	
29	
30	
31	
32	
33	
34	
35	
36	
37	
38	
39	
40	
41	
42	
43	
44	
45	
46	
47	
48	
49	
50	
51	
52	
53	
54	
56	
57	
58	
59	
60	
61	
62	
63	
64	

Material Title	MCAT Subject	Time Spent	# of MCQs or # of Chapters	Times Reviewed	Cost	Note Style	Scores

Note Topic	General Notes
1	
2	
3	
4	
5	
6	
7	
8	
9	
10	
11	
12	
13	
14	
15	
16	
17	
18	
19	
20	
21	
22	
23	
24	
25	
26	
27	
28	
29	
30	
31	
32	
33	
34	
35	
36	
37	
38	
39	
40	
41	
42	
43	
44	
45	
46	
47	
48	
49	
50	
51	
52	
53	
54	
56	
57	
58	
59	
60	
61	
62	
63	
64	

Material Title	MCAT Subject	Time Spent	# of MCQs or # of Chapters	Times Reviewed	Cost	Note Style	Scores

Note Topic	General Notes
1	
2	
3	
4	
5	
6	
7	
8	
9	
10	
11	
12	
13	
14	
15	
16	
17	
18	
19	
20	
21	
22	
23	
24	
25	
26	
27	
28	
29	
30	
31	
32	
33	
34	
35	
36	
37	
38	
39	
40	
41	
42	
43	
44	
45	
46	
47	
48	
49	
50	
51	
52	
53	
54	
56	
57	
58	
59	
60	
61	
62	
63	
64	

Material Title	MCAT Subject	Time Spent	# of MCQs or # of Chapters	Times Reviewed	Cost	Note Style	Scores

Note Topic	General Notes
1	
2	
3	
4	
5	
6	
7	
8	
9	
10	
11	
12	
13	
14	
15	
16	
17	
18	
19	
20	
21	
22	
23	
24	
25	
26	
27	
28	
29	
30	
31	
32	
33	
34	
35	
36	
37	
38	
39	
40	
41	
42	
43	
44	
45	
46	
47	
48	
49	
50	
51	
52	
53	
54	
56	
57	
58	
59	
60	
61	
62	
63	
64	

Material Title	MCAT Subject	Time Spent	# of MCQs or # of Chapters	Times Reviewed	Cost	Note Style	Scores

Note Topic	General Notes
1	
2	
3	
4	
5	
6	
7	
8	
9	
10	
11	
12	
13	
14	
15	
16	
17	
18	
19	
20	
21	
22	
23	
24	
25	
26	
27	
28	
29	
30	
31	
32	
33	
34	
35	
36	
37	
38	
39	
40	
41	
42	
43	
44	
45	
46	
47	
48	
49	
50	
51	
52	
53	
54	
56	
57	
58	
59	
60	
61	
62	
63	
64	

Material Title	MCAT Subject	Time Spent	# of MCQs or # of Chapters	Times Reviewed	Cost	Note Style	Scores

Note Topic	General Notes
1	
2	
3	
4	
5	
6	
7	
8	
9	
10	
11	
12	
13	
14	
15	
16	
17	
18	
19	
20	
21	
22	
23	
24	
25	
26	
27	
28	
29	
30	
31	
32	
33	
34	
35	
36	
37	
38	
39	
40	
41	
42	
43	
44	
45	
46	
47	
48	
49	
50	
51	
52	
53	
54	
56	
57	
58	
59	
60	
61	
62	
63	
64	

Material Title	MCAT Subject	Time Spent	# of MCQs or # of Chapters	Times Reviewed	Cost	Note Style	Scores

Note Topic	General Notes
1	
2	
3	
4	
5	
6	
7	
8	
9	
10	
11	
12	
13	
14	
15	
16	
17	
18	
19	
20	
21	
22	
23	
24	
25	
26	
27	
28	
29	
30	
31	
32	
33	
34	
35	
36	
37	
38	
39	
40	
41	
42	
43	
44	
45	
46	
47	
48	
49	
50	
51	
52	
53	
54	
56	
57	
58	
59	
60	
61	
62	
63	
64	

Material Title	MCAT Subject	Time Spent	# of MCQs or # of Chapters	Times Reviewed	Cost	Note Style	Scores

Note Topic	General Notes
1	
2	
3	
4	
5	
6	
7	
8	
9	
10	
11	
12	
13	
14	
15	
16	
17	
18	
19	
20	
21	
22	
23	
24	
25	
26	
27	
28	
29	
30	
31	
32	
33	
34	
35	
36	
37	
38	
39	
40	
41	
42	
43	
44	
45	
46	
47	
48	
49	
50	
51	
52	
53	
54	
56	
57	
58	
59	
60	
61	
62	
63	
64	

Material Title	MCAT Subject	Time Spent	# of MCQs or # of Chapters	Times Reviewed	Cost	Note Style	Scores

Note Topic	General Notes
1	
2	
3	
4	
5	
6	
7	
8	
9	
10	
11	
12	
13	
14	
15	
16	
17	
18	
19	
20	
21	
22	
23	
24	
25	
26	
27	
28	
29	
30	
31	
32	
33	
34	
35	
36	
37	
38	
39	
40	
41	
42	
43	
44	
45	
46	
47	
48	
49	
50	
51	
52	
53	
54	
56	
57	
58	
59	
60	
61	
62	
63	
64	

Material Title	MCAT Subject	Time Spent	# of MCQs or # of Chapters	Times Reviewed	Cost	Note Style	Scores

Note Topic	General Notes
1	
2	
3	
4	
5	
6	
7	
8	
9	
10	
11	
12	
13	
14	
15	
16	
17	
18	
19	
20	
21	
22	
23	
24	
25	
26	
27	
28	
29	
30	
31	
32	
33	
34	
35	
36	
37	
38	
39	
40	
41	
42	
43	
44	
45	
46	
47	
48	
49	
50	
51	
52	
53	
54	
56	
57	
58	
59	
60	
61	
62	
63	
64	

Material Title	MCAT Subject	Time Spent	# of MCQs or # of Chapters	Times Reviewed	Cost	Note Style	Scores

Note Topic	General Notes
1	
2	
3	
4	
5	
6	
7	
8	
9	
10	
11	
12	
13	
14	
15	
16	
17	
18	
19	
20	
21	
22	
23	
24	
25	
26	
27	
28	
29	
30	
31	
32	
33	
34	
35	
36	
37	
38	
39	
40	
41	
42	
43	
44	
45	
46	
47	
48	
49	
50	
51	
52	
53	
54	
56	
57	
58	
59	
60	
61	
62	
63	
64	

Material Title	MCAT Subject	Time Spent	# of MCQs or # of Chapters	Times Reviewed	Cost	Note Style	Scores

Note Topic	General Notes
1	
2	
3	
4	
5	
6	
7	
8	
9	
10	
11	
12	
13	
14	
15	
16	
17	
18	
19	
20	
21	
22	
23	
24	
25	
26	
27	
28	
29	
30	
31	
32	
33	
34	
35	
36	
37	
38	
39	
40	
41	
42	
43	
44	
45	
46	
47	
48	
49	
50	
51	
52	
53	
54	
56	
57	
58	
59	
60	
61	
62	
63	
64	

Material Title	MCAT Subject	Time Spent	# of MCQs or # of Chapters	Times Reviewed	Cost	Note Style	Scores

Note Topic	General Notes
1	
2	
3	
4	
5	
6	
7	
8	
9	
10	
11	
12	
13	
14	
15	
16	
17	
18	
19	
20	
21	
22	
23	
24	
25	
26	
27	
28	
29	
30	
31	
32	
33	
34	
35	
36	
37	
38	
39	
40	
41	
42	
43	
44	
45	
46	
47	
48	
49	
50	
51	
52	
53	
54	
56	
57	
58	
59	
60	
61	
62	
63	
64	

Material Title	MCAT Subject	Time Spent	# of MCQs or # of Chapters	Times Reviewed	Cost	Note Style	Scores

Note Topic	General Notes
1	
2	
3	
4	
5	
6	
7	
8	
9	
10	
11	
12	
13	
14	
15	
16	
17	
18	
19	
20	
21	
22	
23	
24	
25	
26	
27	
28	
29	
30	
31	
32	
33	
34	
35	
36	
37	
38	
39	
40	
41	
42	
43	
44	
45	
46	
47	
48	
49	
50	
51	
52	
53	
54	
56	
57	
58	
59	
60	
61	
62	
63	
64	

Material Title	MCAT Subject	Time Spent	# of MCQs or # of Chapters	Times Reviewed	Cost	Note Style	Scores

Note Topic	General Notes
1	
2	
3	
4	
5	
6	
7	
8	
9	
10	
11	
12	
13	
14	
15	
16	
17	
18	
19	
20	
21	
22	
23	
24	
25	
26	
27	
28	
29	
30	
31	
32	
33	
34	
35	
36	
37	
38	
39	
40	
41	
42	
43	
44	
45	
46	
47	
48	
49	
50	
51	
52	
53	
54	
56	
57	
58	
59	
60	
61	
62	
63	
64	

Material Title	MCAT Subject	Time Spent	# of MCQs or # of Chapters	Times Reviewed	Cost	Note Style	Scores

Note Topic	General Notes
1	
2	
3	
4	
5	
6	
7	
8	
9	
10	
11	
12	
13	
14	
15	
16	
17	
18	
19	
20	
21	
22	
23	
24	
25	
26	
27	
28	
29	
30	
31	
32	
33	
34	
35	
36	
37	
38	
39	
40	
41	
42	
43	
44	
45	
46	
47	
48	
49	
50	
51	
52	
53	
54	
56	
57	
58	
59	
60	
61	
62	
63	
64	

Material Title	MCAT Subject	Time Spent	# of MCQs or # of Chapters	Times Reviewed	Cost	Note Style	Scores

Note Topic	General Notes
1	
2	
3	
4	
5	
6	
7	
8	
9	
10	
11	
12	
13	
14	
15	
16	
17	
18	
19	
20	
21	
22	
23	
24	
25	
26	
27	
28	
29	
30	
31	
32	
33	
34	
35	
36	
37	
38	
39	
40	
41	
42	
43	
44	
45	
46	
47	
48	
49	
50	
51	
52	
53	
54	
56	
57	
58	
59	
60	
61	
62	
63	
64	

Material Title	MCAT Subject	Time Spent	# of MCQs or # of Chapters	Times Reviewed	Cost	Note Style	Scores

Note Topic	General Notes
1	
2	
3	
4	
5	
6	
7	
8	
9	
10	
11	
12	
13	
14	
15	
16	
17	
18	
19	
20	
21	
22	
23	
24	
25	
26	
27	
28	
29	
30	
31	
32	
33	
34	
35	
36	
37	
38	
39	
40	
41	
42	
43	
44	
45	
46	
47	
48	
49	
50	
51	
52	
53	
54	
56	
57	
58	
59	
60	
61	
62	
63	
64	

Material Title	MCAT Subject	Time Spent	# of MCQs or # of Chapters	Times Reviewed	Cost	Note Style	Scores

Note Topic	General Notes
1	
2	
3	
4	
5	
6	
7	
8	
9	
10	
11	
12	
13	
14	
15	
16	
17	
18	
19	
20	
21	
22	
23	
24	
25	
26	
27	
28	
29	
30	
31	
32	
33	
34	
35	
36	
37	
38	
39	
40	
41	
42	
43	
44	
45	
46	
47	
48	
49	
50	
51	
52	
53	
54	
56	
57	
58	
59	
60	
61	
62	
63	
64	

Material Title	MCAT Subject	Time Spent	# of MCQs or # of Chapters	Times Reviewed	Cost	Note Style	Scores

Note Topic	General Notes
1	
2	
3	
4	
5	
6	
7	
8	
9	
10	
11	
12	
13	
14	
15	
16	
17	
18	
19	
20	
21	
22	
23	
24	
25	
26	
27	
28	
29	
30	
31	
32	
33	
34	
35	
36	
37	
38	
39	
40	
41	
42	
43	
44	
45	
46	
47	
48	
49	
50	
51	
52	
53	
54	
56	
57	
58	
59	
60	
61	
62	
63	
64	

Material Title	MCAT Subject	Time Spent	# of MCQs or # of Chapters	Times Reviewed	Cost	Note Style	Scores

Note Topic	General Notes
1	
2	
3	
4	
5	
6	
7	
8	
9	
10	
11	
12	
13	
14	
15	
16	
17	
18	
19	
20	
21	
22	
23	
24	
25	
26	
27	
28	
29	
30	
31	
32	
33	
34	
35	
36	
37	
38	
39	
40	
41	
42	
43	
44	
45	
46	
47	
48	
49	
50	
51	
52	
53	
54	
56	
57	
58	
59	
60	
61	
62	
63	
64	

Material Title	MCAT Subject	Time Spent	# of MCQs or # of Chapters	Times Reviewed	Cost	Note Style	Scores

Note Topic	General Notes
1	
2	
3	
4	
5	
6	
7	
8	
9	
10	
11	
12	
13	
14	
15	
16	
17	
18	
19	
20	
21	
22	
23	
24	
25	
26	
27	
28	
29	
30	
31	
32	
33	
34	
35	
36	
37	
38	
39	
40	
41	
42	
43	
44	
45	
46	
47	
48	
49	
50	
51	
52	
53	
54	
56	
57	
58	
59	
60	
61	
62	
63	
64	

Material Title	MCAT Subject	Time Spent	# of MCQs or # of Chapters	Times Reviewed	Cost	Note Style	Scores

Note Topic	General Notes
1	
2	
3	
4	
5	
6	
7	
8	
9	
10	
11	
12	
13	
14	
15	
16	
17	
18	
19	
20	
21	
22	
23	
24	
25	
26	
27	
28	
29	
30	
31	
32	
33	
34	
35	
36	
37	
38	
39	
40	
41	
42	
43	
44	
45	
46	
47	
48	
49	
50	
51	
52	
53	
54	
56	
57	
58	
59	
60	
61	
62	
63	
64	

Material Title	MCAT Subject	Time Spent	# of MCQs or # of Chapters	Times Reviewed	Cost	Note Style	Scores

Note Topic	General Notes
1	
2	
3	
4	
5	
6	
7	
8	
9	
10	
11	
12	
13	
14	
15	
16	
17	
18	
19	
20	
21	
22	
23	
24	
25	
26	
27	
28	
29	
30	
31	
32	
33	
34	
35	
36	
37	
38	
39	
40	
41	
42	
43	
44	
45	
46	
47	
48	
49	
50	
51	
52	
53	
54	
56	
57	
58	
59	
60	
61	
62	
63	
64	

Material Title	MCAT Subject	Time Spent	# of MCQs or # of Chapters	Times Reviewed	Cost	Note Style	Scores

Note Topic	General Notes
1	
2	
3	
4	
5	
6	
7	
8	
9	
10	
11	
12	
13	
14	
15	
16	
17	
18	
19	
20	
21	
22	
23	
24	
25	
26	
27	
28	
29	
30	
31	
32	
33	
34	
35	
36	
37	
38	
39	
40	
41	
42	
43	
44	
45	
46	
47	
48	
49	
50	
51	
52	
53	
54	
56	
57	
58	
59	
60	
61	
62	
63	
64	

Material Title	MCAT Subject	Time Spent	# of MCQs or # of Chapters	Times Reviewed	Cost	Note Style	Scores

Note Topic	General Notes
1	
2	
3	
4	
5	
6	
7	
8	
9	
10	
11	
12	
13	
14	
15	
16	
17	
18	
19	
20	
21	
22	
23	
24	
25	
26	
27	
28	
29	
30	
31	
32	
33	
34	
35	
36	
37	
38	
39	
40	
41	
42	
43	
44	
45	
46	
47	
48	
49	
50	
51	
52	
53	
54	
56	
57	
58	
59	
60	
61	
62	
63	
64	

Material Title	MCAT Subject	Time Spent	# of MCQs or # of Chapters	Times Reviewed	Cost	Note Style	Scores

Note Topic	General Notes
1	
2	
3	
4	
5	
6	
7	
8	
9	
10	
11	
12	
13	
14	
15	
16	
17	
18	
19	
20	
21	
22	
23	
24	
25	
26	
27	
28	
29	
30	
31	
32	
33	
34	
35	
36	
37	
38	
39	
40	
41	
42	
43	
44	
45	
46	
47	
48	
49	
50	
51	
52	
53	
54	
56	
57	
58	
59	
60	
61	
62	
63	
64	

Material Title	MCAT Subject	Time Spent	# of MCQs or # of Chapters	Times Reviewed	Cost	Note Style	Scores

Note Topic	General Notes
1	
2	
3	
4	
5	
6	
7	
8	
9	
10	
11	
12	
13	
14	
15	
16	
17	
18	
19	
20	
21	
22	
23	
24	
25	
26	
27	
28	
29	
30	
31	
32	
33	
34	
35	
36	
37	
38	
39	
40	
41	
42	
43	
44	
45	
46	
47	
48	
49	
50	
51	
52	
53	
54	
56	
57	
58	
59	
60	
61	
62	
63	
64	

Material Title	MCAT Subject	Time Spent	# of MCQs or # of Chapters	Times Reviewed	Cost	Note Style	Scores

Note Topic	General Notes
1	
2	
3	
4	
5	
6	
7	
8	
9	
10	
11	
12	
13	
14	
15	
16	
17	
18	
19	
20	
21	
22	
23	
24	
25	
26	
27	
28	
29	
30	
31	
32	
33	
34	
35	
36	
37	
38	
39	
40	
41	
42	
43	
44	
45	
46	
47	
48	
49	
50	
51	
52	
53	
54	
56	
57	
58	
59	
60	
61	
62	
63	
64	

Material Title	MCAT Subject	Time Spent	# of MCQs or # of Chapters	Times Reviewed	Cost	Note Style	Scores

Note Topic	General Notes
1	
2	
3	
4	
5	
6	
7	
8	
9	
10	
11	
12	
13	
14	
15	
16	
17	
18	
19	
20	
21	
22	
23	
24	
25	
26	
27	
28	
29	
30	
31	
32	
33	
34	
35	
36	
37	
38	
39	
40	
41	
42	
43	
44	
45	
46	
47	
48	
49	
50	
51	
52	
53	
54	
56	
57	
58	
59	
60	
61	
62	
63	
64	

Material Title	MCAT Subject	Time Spent	# of MCQs or # of Chapters	Times Reviewed	Cost	Note Style	Scores

Note Topic	General Notes
1	
2	
3	
4	
5	
6	
7	
8	
9	
10	
11	
12	
13	
14	
15	
16	
17	
18	
19	
20	
21	
22	
23	
24	
25	
26	
27	
28	
29	
30	
31	
32	
33	
34	
35	
36	
37	
38	
39	
40	
41	
42	
43	
44	
45	
46	
47	
48	
49	
50	
51	
52	
53	
54	
56	
57	
58	
59	
60	
61	
62	
63	
64	

Material Title	MCAT Subject	Time Spent	# of MCQs or # of Chapters	Times Reviewed	Cost	Note Style	Scores

Note Topic	General Notes
1	
2	
3	
4	
5	
6	
7	
8	
9	
10	
11	
12	
13	
14	
15	
16	
17	
18	
19	
20	
21	
22	
23	
24	
25	
26	
27	
28	
29	
30	
31	
32	
33	
34	
35	
36	
37	
38	
39	
40	
41	
42	
43	
44	
45	
46	
47	
48	
49	
50	
51	
52	
53	
54	
56	
57	
58	
59	
60	
61	
62	
63	
64	

Material Title	MCAT Subject	Time Spent	# of MCQs or # of Chapters	Times Reviewed	Cost	Note Style	Scores

Note Topic	General Notes
1	
2	
3	
4	
5	
6	
7	
8	
9	
10	
11	
12	
13	
14	
15	
16	
17	
18	
19	
20	
21	
22	
23	
24	
25	
26	
27	
28	
29	
30	
31	
32	
33	
34	
35	
36	
37	
38	
39	
40	
41	
42	
43	
44	
45	
46	
47	
48	
49	
50	
51	
52	
53	
54	
56	
57	
58	
59	
60	
61	
62	
63	
64	

Material Title	MCAT Subject	Time Spent	# of MCQs or # of Chapters	Times Reviewed	Cost	Note Style	Scores

Note Topic	General Notes
1	
2	
3	
4	
5	
6	
7	
8	
9	
10	
11	
12	
13	
14	
15	
16	
17	
18	
19	
20	
21	
22	
23	
24	
25	
26	
27	
28	
29	
30	
31	
32	
33	
34	
35	
36	
37	
38	
39	
40	
41	
42	
43	
44	
45	
46	
47	
48	
49	
50	
51	
52	
53	
54	
56	
57	
58	
59	
60	
61	
62	
63	
64	

Material Title	MCAT Subject	Time Spent	# of MCQs or # of Chapters	Times Reviewed	Cost	Note Style	Scores

Note Topic	General Notes
1	
2	
3	
4	
5	
6	
7	
8	
9	
10	
11	
12	
13	
14	
15	
16	
17	
18	
19	
20	
21	
22	
23	
24	
25	
26	
27	
28	
29	
30	
31	
32	
33	
34	
35	
36	
37	
38	
39	
40	
41	
42	
43	
44	
45	
46	
47	
48	
49	
50	
51	
52	
53	
54	
56	
57	
58	
59	
60	
61	
62	
63	
64	

General Full-Length Tracker			Chem/Phys			CARS			Bio/Biochem			Psych/Soc		
	Full-Length Test Title	Date	Score	# Wrong	Time	Score	# Wrong	Time	Score	# Wrong	Time	Score	# Wrong	Time
1														
2														
3														
4														
5														
6														
7														
8														
9														
10														
11														
12														
13														
14														
15														
16														
17														
18														
19														
20														
21														
22														
23														
24														
25														
26														
27														
28														
29														
30														
31														
32														
33														
34														
35														
36														
37														
38														
39														
40														
41														
42														
43														
44														
45														
46														
47														
48														
49														

Full-Length Test Question Analysis	**Chem/Phys**	**CARS**	**Bio/Biochem**	**Psych/Soc**
Title Date	Score # Wrong Time	Score # Wrong Time	Score # Wrong Time	Score # Wrong Time
Q	Chem/Phys Notes	CARS Notes	Bio/Biochem Notes	Psyc/Soc Notes
1				
2				
3				
4				
5				
6				
7				
8				
9				
10				
11				
12				
13				
14				
15				
16				
17				
18				
19				
20				
21				
22				
23				
24				
25				
26				
27				
28				
29				
30				
31				
32				
33				
34				
35				
36				
37				
38				
39				
40				
41				
42				
43				
44				
45				
46				
47				
48				
49				
50				
51				
52				
53				
54				
56				
57				
58				
59				

Full-Length Test Question Analysis	**Chem/Phys**			**CARS**			**Bio/Biochem**			**Psych/Soc**		
Title Date	Score	# Wrong	Time	Score	# Wrong	Time	Score	# Wrong	Time	Score	# Wrong	Time

Q	Chem/Phys Notes	CARS Notes	Bio/Biochem Notes	Psyc/Soc Notes
1				
2				
3				
4				
5				
6				
7				
8				
9				
10				
11				
12				
13				
14				
15				
16				
17				
18				
19				
20				
21				
22				
23				
24				
25				
26				
27				
28				
29				
30				
31				
32				
33				
34				
35				
36				
37				
38				
39				
40				
41				
42				
43				
44				
45				
46				
47				
48				
49				
50				
51				
52				
53				
54				
56				
57				
58				
59				

Full-Length Test Question Analysis	Chem/Phys	CARS	Bio/Biochem	Psych/Soc
Title Date	Score # Wrong Time	Score # Wrong Time	Score # Wrong Time	Score # Wrong Time
Q	Chem/Phys Notes	CARS Notes	Bio/Biochem Notes	Psyc/Soc Notes
1				
2				
3				
4				
5				
6				
7				
8				
9				
10				
11				
12				
13				
14				
15				
16				
17				
18				
19				
20				
21				
22				
23				
24				
25				
26				
27				
28				
29				
30				
31				
32				
33				
34				
35				
36				
37				
38				
39				
40				
41				
42				
43				
44				
45				
46				
47				
48				
49				
50				
51				
52				
53				
54				
56				
57				
58				
59				

Full-Length Test Question Analysis	**Chem/Phys**	**CARS**	**Bio/Biochem**	**Psych/Soc**
Title Date	Score # Wrong Time	Score # Wrong Time	Score # Wrong Time	Score # Wrong Time
Q	Chem/Phys Notes	CARS Notes	Bio/Biochem Notes	Psyc/Soc Notes
1				
2				
3				
4				
5				
6				
7				
8				
9				
10				
11				
12				
13				
14				
15				
16				
17				
18				
19				
20				
21				
22				
23				
24				
25				
26				
27				
28				
29				
30				
31				
32				
33				
34				
35				
36				
37				
38				
39				
40				
41				
42				
43				
44				
45				
46				
47				
48				
49				
50				
51				
52				
53				
54				
56				
57				
58				
59				

Full-Length Test Question Analysis	Chem/Phys			CARS			Bio/Biochem			Psych/Soc		
Title Date	Score	# Wrong	Time	Score	# Wrong	Time	Score	# Wrong	Time	Score	# Wrong	Time
Q	Chem/Phys Notes			CARS Notes			Bio/Biochem Notes			Psyc/Soc Notes		
1												
2												
3												
4												
5												
6												
7												
8												
9												
10												
11												
12												
13												
14												
15												
16												
17												
18												
19												
20												
21												
22												
23												
24												
25												
26												
27												
28												
29												
30												
31												
32												
33												
34												
35												
36												
37												
38												
39												
40												
41												
42												
43												
44												
45												
46												
47												
48												
49												
50												
51												
52												
53												
54												
56												
57												
58												
59												

Full-Length Test Question Analysis	Chem/Phys			CARS			Bio/Biochem			Psych/Soc		
Title Date	Score	# Wrong	Time	Score	# Wrong	Time	Score	# Wrong	Time	Score	# Wrong	Time

Q	Chem/Phys Notes	CARS Notes	Bio/Biochem Notes	Psyc/Soc Notes
1				
2				
3				
4				
5				
6				
7				
8				
9				
10				
11				
12				
13				
14				
15				
16				
17				
18				
19				
20				
21				
22				
23				
24				
25				
26				
27				
28				
29				
30				
31				
32				
33				
34				
35				
36				
37				
38				
39				
40				
41				
42				
43				
44				
45				
46				
47				
48				
49				
50				
51				
52				
53				
54				
56				
57				
58				
59				

Full-Length Test Question Analysis	Chem/Phys			CARS			Bio/Biochem			Psych/Soc		
Title Date	Score	# Wrong	Time	Score	# Wrong	Time	Score	# Wrong	Time	Score	# Wrong	Time
Q	Chem/Phys Notes			CARS Notes			Bio/Biochem Notes			Psyc/Soc Notes		
1												
2												
3												
4												
5												
6												
7												
8												
9												
10												
11												
12												
13												
14												
15												
16												
17												
18												
19												
20												
21												
22												
23												
24												
25												
26												
27												
28												
29												
30												
31												
32												
33												
34												
35												
36												
37												
38												
39												
40												
41												
42												
43												
44												
45												
46												
47												
48												
49												
50												
51												
52												
53												
54												
56												
57												
58												
59												

Full-Length Test Question Analysis	Chem/Phys	CARS	Bio/Biochem	Psych/Soc
Title Date	Score # Wrong Time	Score # Wrong Time	Score # Wrong Time	Score # Wrong Time
Q	Chem/Phys Notes	CARS Notes	Bio/Biochem Notes	Psyc/Soc Notes
1				
2				
3				
4				
5				
6				
7				
8				
9				
10				
11				
12				
13				
14				
15				
16				
17				
18				
19				
20				
21				
22				
23				
24				
25				
26				
27				
28				
29				
30				
31				
32				
33				
34				
35				
36				
37				
38				
39				
40				
41				
42				
43				
44				
45				
46				
47				
48				
49				
50				
51				
52				
53				
54				
56				
57				
58				
59				

Full-Length Test Question Analysis	**Chem/Phys**	**CARS**	**Bio/Biochem**	**Psych/Soc**
Title Date	Score # Wrong Time	Score # Wrong Time	Score # Wrong Time	Score # Wrong Time
Q	Chem/Phys Notes	CARS Notes	Bio/Biochem Notes	Psyc/Soc Notes
1				
2				
3				
4				
5				
6				
7				
8				
9				
10				
11				
12				
13				
14				
15				
16				
17				
18				
19				
20				
21				
22				
23				
24				
25				
26				
27				
28				
29				
30				
31				
32				
33				
34				
35				
36				
37				
38				
39				
40				
41				
42				
43				
44				
45				
46				
47				
48				
49				
50				
51				
52				
53				
54				
56				
57				
58				
59				

Full-Length Test Question Analysis	Chem/Phys	CARS	Bio/Biochem	Psych/Soc
Title Date	Score # Wrong Time	Score # Wrong Time	Score # Wrong Time	Score # Wrong Time
Q	Chem/Phys Notes	CARS Notes	Bio/Biochem Notes	Psyc/Soc Notes
1				
2				
3				
4				
5				
6				
7				
8				
9				
10				
11				
12				
13				
14				
15				
16				
17				
18				
19				
20				
21				
22				
23				
24				
25				
26				
27				
28				
29				
30				
31				
32				
33				
34				
35				
36				
37				
38				
39				
40				
41				
42				
43				
44				
45				
46				
47				
48				
49				
50				
51				
52				
53				
54				
56				
57				
58				
59				

Full-Length Test Question Analysis	Chem/Phys			CARS			Bio/Biochem			Psych/Soc		
Title Date	Score	# Wrong	Time	Score	# Wrong	Time	Score	# Wrong	Time	Score	# Wrong	Time

Q	Chem/Phys Notes	CARS Notes	Bio/Biochem Notes	Psyc/Soc Notes
1				
2				
3				
4				
5				
6				
7				
8				
9				
10				
11				
12				
13				
14				
15				
16				
17				
18				
19				
20				
21				
22				
23				
24				
25				
26				
27				
28				
29				
30				
31				
32				
33				
34				
35				
36				
37				
38				
39				
40				
41				
42				
43				
44				
45				
46				
47				
48				
49				
50				
51				
52				
53				
54				
56				
57				
58				
59				

Full-Length Test Question Analysis	Chem/Phys	CARS	Bio/Biochem	Psych/Soc
Title Date	Score # Wrong Time	Score # Wrong Time	Score # Wrong Time	Score # Wrong Time
Q	Chem/Phys Notes	CARS Notes	Bio/Biochem Notes	Psyc/Soc Notes
1				
2				
3				
4				
5				
6				
7				
8				
9				
10				
11				
12				
13				
14				
15				
16				
17				
18				
19				
20				
21				
22				
23				
24				
25				
26				
27				
28				
29				
30				
31				
32				
33				
34				
35				
36				
37				
38				
39				
40				
41				
42				
43				
44				
45				
46				
47				
48				
49				
50				
51				
52				
53				
54				
56				
57				
58				
59				

Full-Length Test Question Analysis	Chem/Phys	CARS	Bio/Biochem	Psych/Soc
Title Date	Score # Wrong Time	Score # Wrong Time	Score # Wrong Time	Score # Wrong Time
Q	Chem/Phys Notes	CARS Notes	Bio/Biochem Notes	Psyc/Soc Notes
1				
2				
3				
4				
5				
6				
7				
8				
9				
10				
11				
12				
13				
14				
15				
16				
17				
18				
19				
20				
21				
22				
23				
24				
25				
26				
27				
28				
29				
30				
31				
32				
33				
34				
35				
36				
37				
38				
39				
40				
41				
42				
43				
44				
45				
46				
47				
48				
49				
50				
51				
52				
53				
54				
56				
57				
58				
59				

Full-Length Test Question Analysis	Chem/Phys			CARS			Bio/Biochem			Psych/Soc		
Title Date	Score	# Wrong	Time	Score	# Wrong	Time	Score	# Wrong	Time	Score	# Wrong	Time
Q	Chem/Phys Notes			CARS Notes			Bio/Biochem Notes			Psyc/Soc Notes		
1												
2												
3												
4												
5												
6												
7												
8												
9												
10												
11												
12												
13												
14												
15												
16												
17												
18												
19												
20												
21												
22												
23												
24												
25												
26												
27												
28												
29												
30												
31												
32												
33												
34												
35												
36												
37												
38												
39												
40												
41												
42												
43												
44												
45												
46												
47												
48												
49												
50												
51												
52												
53												
54												
56												
57												
58												
59												

Full-Length Test Question Analysis	Chem/Phys			CARS			Bio/Biochem			Psych/Soc		
Title Date	Score	# Wrong	Time	Score	# Wrong	Time	Score	# Wrong	Time	Score	# Wrong	Time
Q	Chem/Phys Notes			CARS Notes			Bio/Biochem Notes			Psyc/Soc Notes		
1												
2												
3												
4												
5												
6												
7												
8												
9												
10												
11												
12												
13												
14												
15												
16												
17												
18												
19												
20												
21												
22												
23												
24												
25												
26												
27												
28												
29												
30												
31												
32												
33												
34												
35												
36												
37												
38												
39												
40												
41												
42												
43												
44												
45												
46												
47												
48												
49												
50												
51												
52												
53												
54												
56												
57												
58												
59												

Full-Length Test Question Analysis	Chem/Phys	CARS	Bio/Biochem	Psych/Soc
Title Date	Score # Wrong Time	Score # Wrong Time	Score # Wrong Time	Score # Wrong Time
Q	Chem/Phys Notes	CARS Notes	Bio/Biochem Notes	Psyc/Soc Notes
1				
2				
3				
4				
5				
6				
7				
8				
9				
10				
11				
12				
13				
14				
15				
16				
17				
18				
19				
20				
21				
22				
23				
24				
25				
26				
27				
28				
29				
30				
31				
32				
33				
34				
35				
36				
37				
38				
39				
40				
41				
42				
43				
44				
45				
46				
47				
48				
49				
50				
51				
52				
53				
54				
56				
57				
58				
59				

Full-Length Test Question Analysis	**Chem/Phys**			**CARS**			**Bio/Biochem**			**Psych/Soc**		
Title Date	Score	# Wrong	Time	Score	# Wrong	Time	Score	# Wrong	Time	Score	# Wrong	Time
Q	Chem/Phys Notes			CARS Notes			Bio/Biochem Notes			Psyc/Soc Notes		
1												
2												
3												
4												
5												
6												
7												
8												
9												
10												
11												
12												
13												
14												
15												
16												
17												
18												
19												
20												
21												
22												
23												
24												
25												
26												
27												
28												
29												
30												
31												
32												
33												
34												
35												
36												
37												
38												
39												
40												
41												
42												
43												
44												
45												
46												
47												
48												
49												
50												
51												
52												
53												
54												
56												
57												
58												
59												

Full-Length Test Question Analysis	Chem/Phys			CARS			Bio/Biochem			Psych/Soc		
Title Date	Score	# Wrong	Time	Score	# Wrong	Time	Score	# Wrong	Time	Score	# Wrong	Time

Q	Chem/Phys Notes	CARS Notes	Bio/Biochem Notes	Psyc/Soc Notes
1				
2				
3				
4				
5				
6				
7				
8				
9				
10				
11				
12				
13				
14				
15				
16				
17				
18				
19				
20				
21				
22				
23				
24				
25				
26				
27				
28				
29				
30				
31				
32				
33				
34				
35				
36				
37				
38				
39				
40				
41				
42				
43				
44				
45				
46				
47				
48				
49				
50				
51				
52				
53				
54				
56				
57				
58				
59				

Full-Length Test Question Analysis	**Chem/Phys**			**CARS**			**Bio/Biochem**			**Psych/Soc**		
Title Date	Score	# Wrong	Time	Score	# Wrong	Time	Score	# Wrong	Time	Score	# Wrong	Time
Q	Chem/Phys Notes			CARS Notes			Bio/Biochem Notes			Psyc/Soc Notes		
1												
2												
3												
4												
5												
6												
7												
8												
9												
10												
11												
12												
13												
14												
15												
16												
17												
18												
19												
20												
21												
22												
23												
24												
25												
26												
27												
28												
29												
30												
31												
32												
33												
34												
35												
36												
37												
38												
39												
40												
41												
42												
43												
44												
45												
46												
47												
48												
49												
50												
51												
52												
53												
54												
56												
57												
58												
59												

Full-Length Test Question Analysis	**Chem/Phys**	**CARS**	**Bio/Biochem**	**Psych/Soc**
Title Date	Score # Wrong Time	Score # Wrong Time	Score # Wrong Time	Score # Wrong Time
Q	Chem/Phys Notes	CARS Notes	Bio/Biochem Notes	Psyc/Soc Notes
1				
2				
3				
4				
5				
6				
7				
8				
9				
10				
11				
12				
13				
14				
15				
16				
17				
18				
19				
20				
21				
22				
23				
24				
25				
26				
27				
28				
29				
30				
31				
32				
33				
34				
35				
36				
37				
38				
39				
40				
41				
42				
43				
44				
45				
46				
47				
48				
49				
50				
51				
52				
53				
54				
56				
57				
58				
59				

Full-Length Test Question Analysis	Chem/Phys			CARS			Bio/Biochem			Psych/Soc		
Title Date	Score	# Wrong	Time	Score	# Wrong	Time	Score	# Wrong	Time	Score	# Wrong	Time
Q	Chem/Phys Notes			CARS Notes			Bio/Biochem Notes			Psyc/Soc Notes		
1												
2												
3												
4												
5												
6												
7												
8												
9												
10												
11												
12												
13												
14												
15												
16												
17												
18												
19												
20												
21												
22												
23												
24												
25												
26												
27												
28												
29												
30												
31												
32												
33												
34												
35												
36												
37												
38												
39												
40												
41												
42												
43												
44												
45												
46												
47												
48												
49												
50												
51												
52												
53												
54												
56												
57												
58												
59												

Full-Length Test Question Analysis	**Chem/Phys**			**CARS**			**Bio/Biochem**			**Psych/Soc**		
Title Date	Score	# Wrong	Time	Score	# Wrong	Time	Score	# Wrong	Time	Score	# Wrong	Time
Q	Chem/Phys Notes			CARS Notes			Bio/Biochem Notes			Psyc/Soc Notes		
1												
2												
3												
4												
5												
6												
7												
8												
9												
10												
11												
12												
13												
14												
15												
16												
17												
18												
19												
20												
21												
22												
23												
24												
25												
26												
27												
28												
29												
30												
31												
32												
33												
34												
35												
36												
37												
38												
39												
40												
41												
42												
43												
44												
45												
46												
47												
48												
49												
50												
51												
52												
53												
54												
56												
57												
58												
59												

Full-Length Test Question Analysis	**Chem/Phys**			**CARS**			**Bio/Biochem**			**Psych/Soc**		
Title Date	Score	# Wrong	Time	Score	# Wrong	Time	Score	# Wrong	Time	Score	# Wrong	Time
Q	Chem/Phys Notes			CARS Notes			Bio/Biochem Notes			Psyc/Soc Notes		
1												
2												
3												
4												
5												
6												
7												
8												
9												
10												
11												
12												
13												
14												
15												
16												
17												
18												
19												
20												
21												
22												
23												
24												
25												
26												
27												
28												
29												
30												
31												
32												
33												
34												
35												
36												
37												
38												
39												
40												
41												
42												
43												
44												
45												
46												
47												
48												
49												
50												
51												
52												
53												
54												
56												
57												
58												
59												

Full-Length Test Question Analysis	Chem/Phys	CARS	Bio/Biochem	Psych/Soc
Title Date	Score # Wrong Time	Score # Wrong Time	Score # Wrong Time	Score # Wrong Time
Q	Chem/Phys Notes	CARS Notes	Bio/Biochem Notes	Psyc/Soc Notes
1				
2				
3				
4				
5				
6				
7				
8				
9				
10				
11				
12				
13				
14				
15				
16				
17				
18				
19				
20				
21				
22				
23				
24				
25				
26				
27				
28				
29				
30				
31				
32				
33				
34				
35				
36				
37				
38				
39				
40				
41				
42				
43				
44				
45				
46				
47				
48				
49				
50				
51				
52				
53				
54				
56				
57				
58				
59				

Full-Length Test Question Analysis	Chem/Phys	CARS	Bio/Biochem	Psych/Soc
Title Date	Score # Wrong Time	Score # Wrong Time	Score # Wrong Time	Score # Wrong Time
Q	Chem/Phys Notes	CARS Notes	Bio/Biochem Notes	Psyc/Soc Notes
1				
2				
3				
4				
5				
6				
7				
8				
9				
10				
11				
12				
13				
14				
15				
16				
17				
18				
19				
20				
21				
22				
23				
24				
25				
26				
27				
28				
29				
30				
31				
32				
33				
34				
35				
36				
37				
38				
39				
40				
41				
42				
43				
44				
45				
46				
47				
48				
49				
50				
51				
52				
53				
54				
56				
57				
58				
59				

Full-Length Test Question Analysis	**Chem/Phys**	**CARS**	**Bio/Biochem**	**Psych/Soc**
Title Date	Score # Wrong Time	Score # Wrong Time	Score # Wrong Time	Score # Wrong Time
Q	Chem/Phys Notes	CARS Notes	Bio/Biochem Notes	Psyc/Soc Notes
1				
2				
3				
4				
5				
6				
7				
8				
9				
10				
11				
12				
13				
14				
15				
16				
17				
18				
19				
20				
21				
22				
23				
24				
25				
26				
27				
28				
29				
30				
31				
32				
33				
34				
35				
36				
37				
38				
39				
40				
41				
42				
43				
44				
45				
46				
47				
48				
49				
50				
51				
52				
53				
54				
56				
57				
58				
59				

Full-Length Test Question Analysis	Chem/Phys	CARS	Bio/Biochem	Psych/Soc
Title Date	Score # Wrong Time	Score # Wrong Time	Score # Wrong Time	Score # Wrong Time
Q	Chem/Phys Notes	CARS Notes	Bio/Biochem Notes	Psyc/Soc Notes
1				
2				
3				
4				
5				
6				
7				
8				
9				
10				
11				
12				
13				
14				
15				
16				
17				
18				
19				
20				
21				
22				
23				
24				
25				
26				
27				
28				
29				
30				
31				
32				
33				
34				
35				
36				
37				
38				
39				
40				
41				
42				
43				
44				
45				
46				
47				
48				
49				
50				
51				
52				
53				
54				
56				
57				
58				
59				

Full-Length Test Question Analysis	Chem/Phys	CARS	Bio/Biochem	Psych/Soc
Title Date	Score # Wrong Time	Score # Wrong Time	Score # Wrong Time	Score # Wrong Time
Q	Chem/Phys Notes	CARS Notes	Bio/Biochem Notes	Psyc/Soc Notes
1				
2				
3				
4				
5				
6				
7				
8				
9				
10				
11				
12				
13				
14				
15				
16				
17				
18				
19				
20				
21				
22				
23				
24				
25				
26				
27				
28				
29				
30				
31				
32				
33				
34				
35				
36				
37				
38				
39				
40				
41				
42				
43				
44				
45				
46				
47				
48				
49				
50				
51				
52				
53				
54				
56				
57				
58				
59				

Full-Length Test Question Analysis	**Chem/Phys**	**CARS**	**Bio/Biochem**	**Psych/Soc**
Title Date	Score # Wrong Time	Score # Wrong Time	Score # Wrong Time	Score # Wrong Time
Q	Chem/Phys Notes	CARS Notes	Bio/Biochem Notes	Psyc/Soc Notes
1				
2				
3				
4				
5				
6				
7				
8				
9				
10				
11				
12				
13				
14				
15				
16				
17				
18				
19				
20				
21				
22				
23				
24				
25				
26				
27				
28				
29				
30				
31				
32				
33				
34				
35				
36				
37				
38				
39				
40				
41				
42				
43				
44				
45				
46				
47				
48				
49				
50				
51				
52				
53				
54				
56				
57				
58				
59				

Full-Length Test Question Analysis	Chem/Phys	CARS	Bio/Biochem	Psych/Soc
Title Date	Score # Wrong Time	Score # Wrong Time	Score # Wrong Time	Score # Wrong Time
Q	Chem/Phys Notes	CARS Notes	Bio/Biochem Notes	Psyc/Soc Notes
1				
2				
3				
4				
5				
6				
7				
8				
9				
10				
11				
12				
13				
14				
15				
16				
17				
18				
19				
20				
21				
22				
23				
24				
25				
26				
27				
28				
29				
30				
31				
32				
33				
34				
35				
36				
37				
38				
39				
40				
41				
42				
43				
44				
45				
46				
47				
48				
49				
50				
51				
52				
53				
54				
56				
57				
58				
59				

Full-Length Test Question Analysis	**Chem/Phys**	**CARS**	**Bio/Biochem**	**Psych/Soc**
Title Date	Score # Wrong Time	Score # Wrong Time	Score # Wrong Time	Score # Wrong Time
Q	Chem/Phys Notes	CARS Notes	Bio/Biochem Notes	Psyc/Soc Notes
1				
2				
3				
4				
5				
6				
7				
8				
9				
10				
11				
12				
13				
14				
15				
16				
17				
18				
19				
20				
21				
22				
23				
24				
25				
26				
27				
28				
29				
30				
31				
32				
33				
34				
35				
36				
37				
38				
39				
40				
41				
42				
43				
44				
45				
46				
47				
48				
49				
50				
51				
52				
53				
54				
56				
57				
58				
59				

Full-Length Test Question Analysis	**Chem/Phys**			**CARS**			**Bio/Biochem**			**Psych/Soc**		
Title Date	Score	# Wrong	Time	Score	# Wrong	Time	Score	# Wrong	Time	Score	# Wrong	Time
Q	Chem/Phys Notes			CARS Notes			Bio/Biochem Notes			Psyc/Soc Notes		
1												
2												
3												
4												
5												
6												
7												
8												
9												
10												
11												
12												
13												
14												
15												
16												
17												
18												
19												
20												
21												
22												
23												
24												
25												
26												
27												
28												
29												
30												
31												
32												
33												
34												
35												
36												
37												
38												
39												
40												
41												
42												
43												
44												
45												
46												
47												
48												
49												
50												
51												
52												
53												
54												
56												
57												
58												
59												

Full-Length Test Question Analysis	**Chem/Phys**	**CARS**	**Bio/Biochem**	**Psych/Soc**
Title Date	Score # Wrong Time	Score # Wrong Time	Score # Wrong Time	Score # Wrong Time
Q	Chem/Phys Notes	CARS Notes	Bio/Biochem Notes	Psyc/Soc Notes
1				
2				
3				
4				
5				
6				
7				
8				
9				
10				
11				
12				
13				
14				
15				
16				
17				
18				
19				
20				
21				
22				
23				
24				
25				
26				
27				
28				
29				
30				
31				
32				
33				
34				
35				
36				
37				
38				
39				
40				
41				
42				
43				
44				
45				
46				
47				
48				
49				
50				
51				
52				
53				
54				
56				
57				
58				
59				

Full-Length Test Question Analysis	**Chem/Phys**	**CARS**	**Bio/Biochem**	**Psych/Soc**
Title Date	Score # Wrong Time	Score # Wrong Time	Score # Wrong Time	Score # Wrong Time
Q	Chem/Phys Notes	CARS Notes	Bio/Biochem Notes	Psyc/Soc Notes
1				
2				
3				
4				
5				
6				
7				
8				
9				
10				
11				
12				
13				
14				
15				
16				
17				
18				
19				
20				
21				
22				
23				
24				
25				
26				
27				
28				
29				
30				
31				
32				
33				
34				
35				
36				
37				
38				
39				
40				
41				
42				
43				
44				
45				
46				
47				
48				
49				
50				
51				
52				
53				
54				
56				
57				
58				
59				

Full-Length Test Question Analysis	Chem/Phys	CARS	Bio/Biochem	Psych/Soc
Title Date	Score # Wrong Time	Score # Wrong Time	Score # Wrong Time	Score # Wrong Time
Q	Chem/Phys Notes	CARS Notes	Bio/Biochem Notes	Psyc/Soc Notes
1				
2				
3				
4				
5				
6				
7				
8				
9				
10				
11				
12				
13				
14				
15				
16				
17				
18				
19				
20				
21				
22				
23				
24				
25				
26				
27				
28				
29				
30				
31				
32				
33				
34				
35				
36				
37				
38				
39				
40				
41				
42				
43				
44				
45				
46				
47				
48				
49				
50				
51				
52				
53				
54				
56				
57				
58				
59				

Full-Length Test Question Analysis	**Chem/Phys**	**CARS**	**Bio/Biochem**	**Psych/Soc**
Title Date	Score # Wrong Time	Score # Wrong Time	Score # Wrong Time	Score # Wrong Time
Q	Chem/Phys Notes	CARS Notes	Bio/Biochem Notes	Psyc/Soc Notes
1				
2				
3				
4				
5				
6				
7				
8				
9				
10				
11				
12				
13				
14				
15				
16				
17				
18				
19				
20				
21				
22				
23				
24				
25				
26				
27				
28				
29				
30				
31				
32				
33				
34				
35				
36				
37				
38				
39				
40				
41				
42				
43				
44				
45				
46				
47				
48				
49				
50				
51				
52				
53				
54				
56				
57				
58				
59				

Full-Length Test Question Analysis	Chem/Phys	CARS	Bio/Biochem	Psych/Soc
Title Date	Score # Wrong Time	Score # Wrong Time	Score # Wrong Time	Score # Wrong Time
Q	Chem/Phys Notes	CARS Notes	Bio/Biochem Notes	Psyc/Soc Notes
1				
2				
3				
4				
5				
6				
7				
8				
9				
10				
11				
12				
13				
14				
15				
16				
17				
18				
19				
20				
21				
22				
23				
24				
25				
26				
27				
28				
29				
30				
31				
32				
33				
34				
35				
36				
37				
38				
39				
40				
41				
42				
43				
44				
45				
46				
47				
48				
49				
50				
51				
52				
53				
54				
56				
57				
58				
59				

Full-Length Test Question Analysis	Chem/Phys			CARS			Bio/Biochem			Psych/Soc		
Title Date	Score	# Wrong	Time	Score	# Wrong	Time	Score	# Wrong	Time	Score	# Wrong	Time

Q	Chem/Phys Notes	CARS Notes	Bio/Biochem Notes	Psyc/Soc Notes
1				
2				
3				
4				
5				
6				
7				
8				
9				
10				
11				
12				
13				
14				
15				
16				
17				
18				
19				
20				
21				
22				
23				
24				
25				
26				
27				
28				
29				
30				
31				
32				
33				
34				
35				
36				
37				
38				
39				
40				
41				
42				
43				
44				
45				
46				
47				
48				
49				
50				
51				
52				
53				
54				
56				
57				
58				
59				

Full-Length Test Question Analysis	Chem/Phys	CARS	Bio/Biochem	Psych/Soc
Title Date	Score # Wrong Time	Score # Wrong Time	Score # Wrong Time	Score # Wrong Time
Q	Chem/Phys Notes	CARS Notes	Bio/Biochem Notes	Psyc/Soc Notes
1				
2				
3				
4				
5				
6				
7				
8				
9				
10				
11				
12				
13				
14				
15				
16				
17				
18				
19				
20				
21				
22				
23				
24				
25				
26				
27				
28				
29				
30				
31				
32				
33				
34				
35				
36				
37				
38				
39				
40				
41				
42				
43				
44				
45				
46				
47				
48				
49				
50				
51				
52				
53				
54				
56				
57				
58				
59				

Full-Length Test Question Analysis	Chem/Phys	CARS	Bio/Biochem	Psych/Soc
Title Date	Score # Wrong Time	Score # Wrong Time	Score # Wrong Time	Score # Wrong Time
Q	Chem/Phys Notes	CARS Notes	Bio/Biochem Notes	Psyc/Soc Notes
1				
2				
3				
4				
5				
6				
7				
8				
9				
10				
11				
12				
13				
14				
15				
16				
17				
18				
19				
20				
21				
22				
23				
24				
25				
26				
27				
28				
29				
30				
31				
32				
33				
34				
35				
36				
37				
38				
39				
40				
41				
42				
43				
44				
45				
46				
47				
48				
49				
50				
51				
52				
53				
54				
56				
57				
58				
59				

Full-Length Test Question Analysis	**Chem/Phys**	**CARS**	**Bio/Biochem**	**Psych/Soc**
Title Date	Score # Wrong Time	Score # Wrong Time	Score # Wrong Time	Score # Wrong Time
Q	Chem/Phys Notes	CARS Notes	Bio/Biochem Notes	Psyc/Soc Notes
1				
2				
3				
4				
5				
6				
7				
8				
9				
10				
11				
12				
13				
14				
15				
16				
17				
18				
19				
20				
21				
22				
23				
24				
25				
26				
27				
28				
29				
30				
31				
32				
33				
34				
35				
36				
37				
38				
39				
40				
41				
42				
43				
44				
45				
46				
47				
48				
49				
50				
51				
52				
53				
54				
56				
57				
58				
59				

Full-Length Test Question Analysis	Chem/Phys			CARS			Bio/Biochem			Psych/Soc		
Title Date	Score	# Wrong	Time	Score	# Wrong	Time	Score	# Wrong	Time	Score	# Wrong	Time

Q	Chem/Phys Notes	CARS Notes	Bio/Biochem Notes	Psyc/Soc Notes
1				
2				
3				
4				
5				
6				
7				
8				
9				
10				
11				
12				
13				
14				
15				
16				
17				
18				
19				
20				
21				
22				
23				
24				
25				
26				
27				
28				
29				
30				
31				
32				
33				
34				
35				
36				
37				
38				
39				
40				
41				
42				
43				
44				
45				
46				
47				
48				
49				
50				
51				
52				
53				
54				
56				
57				
58				
59				

Full-Length Test Question Analysis	Chem/Phys			CARS			Bio/Biochem			Psych/Soc		
Title Date	Score	# Wrong	Time	Score	# Wrong	Time	Score	# Wrong	Time	Score	# Wrong	Time

Q	Chem/Phys Notes	CARS Notes	Bio/Biochem Notes	Psyc/Soc Notes
1				
2				
3				
4				
5				
6				
7				
8				
9				
10				
11				
12				
13				
14				
15				
16				
17				
18				
19				
20				
21				
22				
23				
24				
25				
26				
27				
28				
29				
30				
31				
32				
33				
34				
35				
36				
37				
38				
39				
40				
41				
42				
43				
44				
45				
46				
47				
48				
49				
50				
51				
52				
53				
54				
56				
57				
58				
59				

Full-Length Test Question Analysis	Chem/Phys			CARS			Bio/Biochem			Psych/Soc		
Title Date	Score	# Wrong	Time	Score	# Wrong	Time	Score	# Wrong	Time	Score	# Wrong	Time
Q	Chem/Phys Notes			CARS Notes			Bio/Biochem Notes			Psyc/Soc Notes		
1												
2												
3												
4												
5												
6												
7												
8												
9												
10												
11												
12												
13												
14												
15												
16												
17												
18												
19												
20												
21												
22												
23												
24												
25												
26												
27												
28												
29												
30												
31												
32												
33												
34												
35												
36												
37												
38												
39												
40												
41												
42												
43												
44												
45												
46												
47												
48												
49												
50												
51												
52												
53												
54												
56												
57												
58												
59												

Full-Length Test Question Analysis	Chem/Phys			CARS			Bio/Biochem			Psych/Soc		
Title Date	Score	# Wrong	Time	Score	# Wrong	Time	Score	# Wrong	Time	Score	# Wrong	Time
Q	Chem/Phys Notes			CARS Notes			Bio/Biochem Notes			Psyc/Soc Notes		
1												
2												
3												
4												
5												
6												
7												
8												
9												
10												
11												
12												
13												
14												
15												
16												
17												
18												
19												
20												
21												
22												
23												
24												
25												
26												
27												
28												
29												
30												
31												
32												
33												
34												
35												
36												
37												
38												
39												
40												
41												
42												
43												
44												
45												
46												
47												
48												
49												
50												
51												
52												
53												
54												
56												
57												
58												
59												

Full-Length Test Question Analysis	Chem/Phys			CARS			Bio/Biochem			Psych/Soc		
Title Date	Score	# Wrong	Time	Score	# Wrong	Time	Score	# Wrong	Time	Score	# Wrong	Time

Q	Chem/Phys Notes	CARS Notes	Bio/Biochem Notes	Psyc/Soc Notes
1				
2				
3				
4				
5				
6				
7				
8				
9				
10				
11				
12				
13				
14				
15				
16				
17				
18				
19				
20				
21				
22				
23				
24				
25				
26				
27				
28				
29				
30				
31				
32				
33				
34				
35				
36				
37				
38				
39				
40				
41				
42				
43				
44				
45				
46				
47				
48				
49				
50				
51				
52				
53				
54				
56				
57				
58				
59				

Full-Length Test Question Analysis	Chem/Phys	CARS	Bio/Biochem	Psych/Soc
Title Date	Score # Wrong Time	Score # Wrong Time	Score # Wrong Time	Score # Wrong Time
Q	Chem/Phys Notes	CARS Notes	Bio/Biochem Notes	Psyc/Soc Notes
1				
2				
3				
4				
5				
6				
7				
8				
9				
10				
11				
12				
13				
14				
15				
16				
17				
18				
19				
20				
21				
22				
23				
24				
25				
26				
27				
28				
29				
30				
31				
32				
33				
34				
35				
36				
37				
38				
39				
40				
41				
42				
43				
44				
45				
46				
47				
48				
49				
50				
51				
52				
53				
54				
56				
57				
58				
59				

Full-Length Test Question Analysis	Chem/Phys			CARS			Bio/Biochem			Psych/Soc		
Title Date	Score	# Wrong	Time	Score	# Wrong	Time	Score	# Wrong	Time	Score	# Wrong	Time

Q	Chem/Phys Notes	CARS Notes	Bio/Biochem Notes	Psyc/Soc Notes
1				
2				
3				
4				
5				
6				
7				
8				
9				
10				
11				
12				
13				
14				
15				
16				
17				
18				
19				
20				
21				
22				
23				
24				
25				
26				
27				
28				
29				
30				
31				
32				
33				
34				
35				
36				
37				
38				
39				
40				
41				
42				
43				
44				
45				
46				
47				
48				
49				
50				
51				
52				
53				
54				
56				
57				
58				
59				

Full-Length Test Question Analysis	Chem/Phys	CARS	Bio/Biochem	Psych/Soc
Title Date	Score # Wrong Time	Score # Wrong Time	Score # Wrong Time	Score # Wrong Time
Q	Chem/Phys Notes	CARS Notes	Bio/Biochem Notes	Psyc/Soc Notes
1				
2				
3				
4				
5				
6				
7				
8				
9				
10				
11				
12				
13				
14				
15				
16				
17				
18				
19				
20				
21				
22				
23				
24				
25				
26				
27				
28				
29				
30				
31				
32				
33				
34				
35				
36				
37				
38				
39				
40				
41				
42				
43				
44				
45				
46				
47				
48				
49				
50				
51				
52				
53				
54				
56				
57				
58				
59				

Full-Length Test Question Analysis	**Chem/Phys**			**CARS**			**Bio/Biochem**			**Psych/Soc**		
Title Date	Score	# Wrong	Time	Score	# Wrong	Time	Score	# Wrong	Time	Score	# Wrong	Time
Q	Chem/Phys Notes			CARS Notes			Bio/Biochem Notes			Psyc/Soc Notes		
1												
2												
3												
4												
5												
6												
7												
8												
9												
10												
11												
12												
13												
14												
15												
16												
17												
18												
19												
20												
21												
22												
23												
24												
25												
26												
27												
28												
29												
30												
31												
32												
33												
34												
35												
36												
37												
38												
39												
40												
41												
42												
43												
44												
45												
46												
47												
48												
49												
50												
51												
52												
53												
54												
56												
57												
58												
59												

Course GPA Tracker							
	Major:		Overall GPA:		Science GPA:		College(s):
	Course Title	Semester/ Quarter	Premed Req	Degree Req	MCAT Req	GPA	Notes
1							
2							
3							
4							
5							
6							
7							
8							
9							
10							
11							
12							
13							
14							
15							
16							
17							
18							
19							
20							
21							
22							
23							
24							
25							
26							
27							
28							
29							
30							
31							
32							
33							
34							
35							
36							
37							
38							
39							
40							
41							
42							
43							
44							
45							
46							
47							
48							
49							
50							
51							
52							
53							
Tips							**Aim for a 4.0 in all courses if possible to make leeway for potentially unpreventable low grades. Have a thorough reason for lower grades. Have friends who score high to increase odds and own ability to score high. Always get a tutor if you do not understand a topic. Use Quizlet to memorize facts. Find and finish 6+ practice tests from a similar course to simulate test taking. Always be prepared 1-2 days in advance for any test. You can do this!**

Letters of Recommendation							
	Name	Phone	Email	Profession	Relationship	Submitted?	What should they write about?
1							
2							
3							
4							
5							
6							
7							
8							
9							
10							
11							
12							
13							
14							
15							
16							
17							
18							
19							
20							
21							
22							
23							
24							

Tips

1. You need a minimum of 3 letters from science professors who taught and graded you (aim for A-scoring professors or those you have spoken with).
2. Make sure to contact your premed office to see if a premed committee letter is required (meet your premed advisor 2-4 times a year)
3. Have a LOR from any and all research advisors if your did research
4. Have a LOR from any and all doctors you have shadowed or who know you
5. It is okay for an LOR writer to say no. This is better than convincing them to do it. All LORS must sound over the top and superb as this is now the norm for apps.
6. LOR writers are very busy. Remind them or set up a time to sit down with them to help them put aside time to draft it.
7. If an LOR writer asks you to write it, be professional and write from their perspective. View samples and have it checked.
8. Set up a bullet point list of your activities for them to glance at the write the LOR
9. Make sure each school receives the LORS! They are specific and all must be manually added per school.
10. You do not need LORS to submit the medical school application but they will delay your review if late.

Work and Activities	
1	
Experience Type	
Experience Name	
Experience Dates (Hrs/Week)	
Organization Name/Location	
Contact Title- Full Name, Job Title, Phone, & Email	
Notes about experience- Roles, Stories, Etc	
2	
Experience Type	
Experience Name	
Experience Dates (Hrs/Week)	
Organization Name/Location	
Contact Title- Full Name, Job Title, Phone, & Email	
Notes about experience- Roles, Stories, Etc	
3	
Experience Type	
Experience Name	
Experience Dates (Hrs/Week)	
Organization Name/Location	
Contact Title- Full Name, Job Title, Phone, & Email	
Notes about experience- Roles, Stories, Etc	
4	
Experience Type	
Experience Name	
Experience Dates (Hrs/Week)	
Organization Name/Location	
Contact Title- Full Name, Job Title, Phone, & Email	
Notes about experience- Roles, Stories, Etc	
5	
Experience Type	
Experience Name	
Experience Dates (Hrs/Week)	
Organization Name/Location	
Contact Title- Full Name, Job Title, Phone, & Email	
Notes about experience- Roles, Stories, Etc	

6	
Experience Type	
Experience Name	
Experience Dates (Hrs/Week)	
Organization Name/Location	
Contact Title- Full Name, Job Title, Phone, & Email	
Notes about experience- Roles, Stories, Etc	
7	
Experience Type	
Experience Name	
Experience Dates (Hrs/Week)	
Organization Name/Location	
Contact Title- Full Name, Job Title, Phone, & Email	
Notes about experience- Roles, Stories, Etc	
8	
Experience Type	
Experience Name	
Experience Dates (Hrs/Week)	
Organization Name/Location	
Contact Title- Full Name, Job Title, Phone, & Email	
Notes about experience- Roles, Stories, Etc	
9	
Experience Type	
Experience Name	
Experience Dates (Hrs/Week)	
Organization Name/Location	
Contact Title- Full Name, Job Title, Phone, & Email	
Notes about experience- Roles, Stories, Etc	
10	
Experience Type	
Experience Name	
Experience Dates (Hrs/Week)	
Organization Name/Location	
Contact Title- Full Name, Job Title, Phone, & Email	
Notes about experience- Roles, Stories, Etc	

11	
Experience Type	
Experience Name	
Experience Dates (Hrs/Week)	
Organization Name/Location	
Contact Title- Full Name, Job Title, Phone, & Email	
Notes about experience- Roles, Stories, Etc	
12	
Experience Type	
Experience Name	
Experience Dates (Hrs/Week)	
Organization Name/Location	
Contact Title- Full Name, Job Title, Phone, & Email	
Notes about experience- Roles, Stories, Etc	
13	
Experience Type	
Experience Name	
Experience Dates (Hrs/Week)	
Organization Name/Location	
Contact Title- Full Name, Job Title, Phone, & Email	
Notes about experience- Roles, Stories, Etc	
14	
Experience Type	
Experience Name	
Experience Dates (Hrs/Week)	
Organization Name/Location	
Contact Title- Full Name, Job Title, Phone, & Email	
Notes about experience- Roles, Stories, Etc	
15	
Experience Type	
Experience Name	
Experience Dates (Hrs/Week)	
Organization Name/Location	
Contact Title- Full Name, Job Title, Phone, & Email	
Notes about experience- Roles, Stories, Etc	

Tips	You can fit up to 15 work/activities in an M.D. application with a character limit of 700 (up to 4 "times" for each). Please be concise on what you did. Making it shorter (while still informative) gives your interviewer a better chance to actually skim and read all of it properly. Medical schools prefer you have enough experiences to fill up these 15. It is not the "length" that matter, it is how you learned from it. 3 of these experiences are "the most meaningful" which means you have another 1325 characters to explain why or what you did for it to be meaningful. It is OKAY to fit in more than one"experience"under 1 of the 15 if you have too many (IE"Hospital Experience" and list each different hospital as a new occurrence) but prioritize filling up 15 first. It is flexible. Include EVERYTHING that could possible show that you will make a great doctor. Even working at an icecream shop! But remember: some medical schools are still "traditional". Be careful about mentioning work/activities that may be meaningful to you, but are not reflected well with traditional interviewers. The AMCAS will arrange this in a timeline. They WILL see gaps in work/activities, make sure there are no gaps without a reason as to why. Do your best to have 15 work/activities. You are being compared to students (regardless of age), you need to make sure your application shows commitment and well-roundness. General Application tip: There are different applications for D.O. schools and Texas Medical Schools. Apply to both if your prefer them, if your GPA is lower, MCAT is lower, etc. Use the start class website to determine which are best to apply for. Save experience type, name, dates, average hours/week, organization name, location, contact full name/title/ phone/email, and a brief list of what you did for each work/activity. Medical schools sometimes will call or email to verify. Categories: Paid employment (not military), Paid employment (military), Community service/volunteer (not medical/ clinical), Community service/volunteer (medical/clinical), Research/lab, Teaching/tutoring, Honors/awards/recognition's, Conferences attended, Presentations/posters, Publications, Extracurricular/hobbies/avocations, Leadership (not listed elsewhere), Intercollegiate athletics, Artistic endeavors, Others.

Medical School Application & Selection													
	Medical School	Avg. MCAT	Avg. GPA	Personal Rank	Secondary Received	Cost	Interview Received	Interview Style	Interview Date	Cost	Thank you Card Sent	Accepted	Details
1													
2													
3													
4													
5													
6													
7													
8													
9													
10													
11													
12													
13													
14													
15													
16													
17													
18													
19													
20													
21													
22													
23													
24													
25													
26													
27													
28													
29													
30													
31													
32													
33													
34													
35													
36													
37													
38													
39													
40													
41													
42													
43													
44													
45													
46													
47													
48													
49													
50													
51													
52													
53													
54													
55													
56													
57													
58													
59													
60													
61													

1.Pick the number of schools you can afford and increase number of schools **(students apply from 10 to 60+ schools)** if you feel your application feeling "lacking".
2.Financial waivers are available! It costs about $25 per school after the first school. Secondaries range from $50-100. Interviews (flights, hotels, etc) will cost much most unless they are local. To get your application submitted FAST, just add a single school that you may not even be able to get accepted to so your application without MCAT or LORS still gets processed faster.
3.Medical schools do not see the number of schools you apply to. Apply smart. Apply to school's whose location you may have ties with. Apply to schools whose GPA and MCAT are around yours. Apply to schools with a low,medium,and high level of acceptance(distribute so more schools with high level of acceptance are added).
4.Verify LOR and premed course requirements of every school. Verify application send in date (Application opens early May and earliest submissions are in June of JUNIOR YEAR or 1 year before you want to go).
5. You can apply as late as September. Submitting the AMCAS in early June/late august will process it faster (submitting in July can take up to 5 weeks sometimes!).
6.Double check the categories your courses are in and hours. Make sure ALL transcripts are sent to AMCAS! Messing up on this might affect your application processing time. Not informing about transcripts can take away your medical school acceptance.
7. EXPLAIN C grades and withdrawals if asked for. Do not mention them unless there is a serious trend and VALID reason (overwhelmed or too difficult is not a valid reason). 8. Be ready to explain gap years and gaps in activities accordingly.
9. Google schools on their website (outside of ranking). Even the top 10 schools might not be a "good fit" for you. Always choose the school that will support YOU to become the best doctor to can. Some schools are research and some are patient- based.
Medical School Ranking: http://medical-schools.startclass.com/

100 Medical School Interview Practice Questions
Adapted from University of Colorado at Boulder
Please review online resources to find more in the case that you have more time to prepare.

Question	Response
1. What are your career plans and what led you to these decisions?	
2. What do you feel is the purpose of Medical School?	
3. Tell me about why you are interested in this program.	
4. Describe your style of communicating and interacting with others. Give an example of a situation in which you had to utilize effective interpersonal skills.	
5. Describe a situation in which you were dependable or demonstrated initiative. One in which you were not as dependable as you would have liked.	
6. What experiences have you had working with diverse populations?	
7. How do you handle stress?	
8. From what you understand of medical school, what part of the program will be most difficult for you?	
9. If you were a cookie, what cookie would you be?	
10. Describe how you can effectively deal with someone in crisis.	
11. What was your favorite college course and why?	
12. What do you hope to gain from this experience?	
13. Describe your style of communicating and interacting with others.	
14. Tell me about a time when you demonstrated initiative.	
15. Tell me about a time when you faced a conflict or anger with another individual.	
16. Tell me about a time when you were criticized unfairly.	
17. Tell me about a time when you failed.	
18. How do you handle failure?	
19. Tell me about a time when you've been disappointed in a teammate or fellow group member. What happened? How did you approach the situation?	
20. Describe a situation in which you have worked with a diverse group of people. What did you learn from that situation?	
21. How do you handle change?	
22. How do you go about making important decisions?	
23. If you could start your college career all over again, what would you do differently?	
24. What were your most memorable accomplishments in your college career?	
25. What does the word "success" mean to you?	
26. What attracted you to this program?	

27. What do you do when you are not at work or school?	
28. How would your teammates describe you? How would your professors describe you?	
29. If we contacted your references now, what do you think they would say about you?	
30. If you could change one aspect of your personality with a snap of your fingers, what would you change?	
31. In what course did you get the worst grades? Why?	
32. What two things would you consider your greatest strengths?	
33. What two things would you consider your greatest weaknesses?	
34. What else do you want us to know about you before you leave today?	
35. Who would you say has been the most influential person in the last one-hundred years?	
36. Why do you want to be a doctor?	
37. What do you do in your spare time?	
38. What are your specific goals in medicine?	
39. What stimulated your interest in medicine?	
40. What do you think about HMO's and the changes taking place in medicine?	
41. What schools have you applied to?	
42. What do you intend to gain from a medical education?	
43. What do you think about euthanasia?	
44. Why do you think so many people want to be doctors?	
45. Do you think a physician should tell a patient he/she has eight months to live?	
46. There are 1,000 applicants as qualified as you. Why should we pick you?	
47. What steps have you taken to acquaint yourself with what a physician does?	
48. How would your plans differ if you knew that all physicians would be working in HMO's in the future?	
49. What do you think is the most pressing issue in medicine today?	
50. What will you do if you don't get into medical school?	
51. What are your positive qualities and what are your shortcomings?	
52. What is your relationship with your family?	
53. How do you think your role as a physician fits in with your role as a member of the community?	
54. Describe your personality.	
55. What do you have to offer our school?	

56. What are the best and worst things that have ever happened to you?	
57. What do you see yourself doing in medicine 10-15 years from now?	
58. Is medicine a rewarding experience? Why?	
59. Would you practice in the inner city? What do you think happens to people who practice medicine there (attitude changes, etc.)?	
60. If there were an accident on the highway, would you stop and help the victims, knowing that doing so might lead to a malpractice claim against you?	
61. What aspects of your life's experiences do you think make you a good candidate for medical school?	
62. If your best friends were asked to describe you, what would they say?	
63. How do you plan to finance your medical education?	
64. What do you think about the ongoing conflict in Iraq?	
65. Discuss a book that you have recently read for pleasure. Why did you select that book?	
66. If you could invite four people to dinner, who would they be? Why?	
67. A patient who has been in an accident needs a blood transfusion. She states that her religion does not allow them. You are the physician in charge. What will you do? Will you override her strong objection? Why/why not?	
68. If you have the choice of giving a transplant to a successful elderly member of the community or a 20-year old drug addict, how do you choose?	
69. What will you do if you are not accepted to medical school this year?	
70. What newspapers, journals, etc., do you read on a regular basis?	
71. Why did you choose your undergraduate major?	
72. What extracurricular activities were you involved in during your undergraduate major?	
73. What qualities do you look for in a physician?	
74. Where do we stand in your list of medical school preferences?	
75. What is the most pressing health issue today?	
76. What experiences have you had in community involvement that demonstrate your commitment to medicine?	
77. How do you think your personal background will affect your practice?	
78. What are the negative aspects of medicine from a professional standpoint?	
79. Would you like academic medicine as a career?	
80. How might you deal with a terminally ill patient?	
81. If you want to help people, why not social work?	
82. Describe any travels that you have undertaken and exposure to other cultures than your own, if any.	
83. Do you prefer the idea of basic research or of working with people?	

84. Have you an alternative career plan?	
85. When you need counseling for personal problems, whom do you talk with?	
86. Describe your childhood and present living conditions.	
87. How will you keep in touch with community needs?	
88. How do you handle blood and gore?	
89. Tell us your opinion of this medical school's curriculum.	
90. Discuss National Health Insurance and how it would affect the physician and the patient.	
91. Do you feel that medical students receiving federal loans should spend time practicing medicine in a rural area to give society something in return?	
92. What are the differences between Britain's health care delivery system and ours?	
93. What is the biggest problem in the world today?	
94. What is your solution to terrorism?	
95. How do you feel about euthanasia?	
96. What is success?	
97. What do you think about American primary health care delivery (i.e., status quo, total private systems, national health insurance)?	
98. If you discovered a classmate cheating, what would you do?	
99. Tell me about your family. How do they feel about your decision to attend medical school?	
100. What impact do you want to have on the medical profession?	

□ Section 1: Biological and Biochemical Foundations of Living Systems			
□ Foundational Concept 1: Biomolecules have unique properties that determine how they contribute to the structure and function of cells and how they participate in the processes necessary to maintain life.			
□ **1A. Structure and function of proteins and their constituent amino acids**	□ Amino Acids (BC, OC)	□ Description	□ Absolute configuration at the α position □ Amino acids as dipolarions □ Classifications □ Acidic or basic □ Hydrophobic or hydrophilic
		□ Reactions	□ Sulfur linkage for cysteine and cysteine □ Peptide linkage: polypeptides and proteins □ Hydrolysis
	□Protein Structure (BIO, BC, OC)	□ Structure	□ 1° structure of proteins □ 2° structure of proteins □ 3° structure of proteins; role of proline, cystine, hydrophobic bonding □ 4° structure of proteins (BIO, BC)
		□ Conformational stability	□ Denaturing and folding □ Hydrophobic interactions □ Solvation layer (entropy) (BC)
		□ Separation techniques	□ Isoelectric point □ Electrophoresis
	□ Non-Enzymatic Protein Function (BIO, BC)	□ Binding (BC)	
		□ Immune system	
		□ Motors	
	□ Enzyme Structure and Function (BIO, BC)	□ Function of enzymes in catalyzing biological reactions	
		□ Enzyme classification by reaction type	
		□ Reduction of activation energy	
		□ Substrates and enzyme specificity	
		□ Active Site Model	
		□ Induced-fit Model	
		□ Mechanism of catalysis	□ Cofactors □ Coenzymes □ Water-soluble vitamins
		□ Effects of local conditions on enzyme activity	
	□ Control of Enzyme Activity (BIO, BC)	□ Kinetics	□ General (catalysis) □ Michaelis-Menten □ Cooperativity
		□ Feedback regulation	
		□ Inhibition - types	□ Competitive □ Non-competitive □ Mixed (BC) □ Uncompetitive (BC)
		□ Regulatory enzymes	□ Allosteric enzymes □ Covalently-modified enzymes □ Zymogen
□ **1B. Transmission of genetic information from the gene to the protein**□	□ Nucleic Acid Structure and Function (BIO, BC)	□ Description	
		□ Nucleotides and nucleosides	□ Sugar phosphate backbone □ Pyrimidine, purine residues
		□ Deoxyribonucleic acid (DNA): double helix, Watson-Crick model of DNA structure	
		□ Base pairing specificity: A with T, G with C	
		□ Function in transmission of genetic information (BIO)	
		□ DNA denaturation, reannealing, hybridization	
	□ DNA Replication (BIO)	□ Mechanism of replication: separation of strands, specific coupling of free nucleic acids	
		□ Semi-conservative nature of replication	
		□ Specific enzymes involved in replication	
		□ Origins of replication, multiple origins in eukaryotes	
		□ Replicating the ends of DNA molecules	
	□ Repair of DNA (BIO)	□ Repair during replication	
		□ Repair of mutation	
	□ Genetic Code (BIO)	□ Central Dogma: DNA → RNA → protein	
		□ The triplet code	
		□ Codon-anticodon relationship	
		□ Degenerate code, wobble pairing	
		□ Missense, nonsense codons	
		□ Initiation, termination codons	
		□ Messenger RNA (mRNA)	
	□ Transcription (BIO)	□ Transfer RNA (tRNA); ribosomal RNA (rRNA)	
		□ Mechanism of transcription	
		□ mRNA processing in eukaryotes, introns, exons	
		□ Ribozymes, spliceosomes, small nuclear ribonucleoproteins (snRNPs), small nuclear RNAs (snRNAs)	
		□ Functional and evolutionary importance of introns	
	□ Translation (BIO)	□ Roles of mRNA, tRNA, rRNA	
		□ Role and structure of ribosomes	
		□ Initiation, termination co-factors	
		□ Post-translational modification of proteins	
	□ Eukaryotic Chromosome Organization (BIO)	□ Chromosomal proteins	
		□ Single copy vs. repetitive DNA	
		□ Supercoiling	
		□ Heterochromatin vs. euchromatin	
		□ Telomeres, centromeres	
	□ Control of Gene Expression in Prokaryotes (BIO)	□ Operon Concept, Jacob-Monod Model	
		□ Gene repression in bacteria	
		□ Positive control in bacteria	
	□ Control of Gene Expression in Eukaryotes (BIO)	□ Transcriptional regulation	
		□ DNA binding proteins, transcription factors	
		□ Gene amplification and duplication	
		□ Post-transcriptional control, basic concept of splicing (introns, exons)	
		□ Cancer as a failure of normal cellular controls, oncogenes, tumor suppressor genes	

		□ Regulation of chromatin structure	
		□ DNA methylation	
		□ Role of non-coding RNAs	
	□ Recombinant DNA and Biotechnology (BIO)	□ Gene cloning	
		□ Restriction enzymes	
		□ DNA libraries	
		□ Generation of cDNA	
		□ Hybridization	
		□ Expressing cloned genes	
		□ Polymerase chain reaction	
		□ Gel electrophoresis and Southern blotting	
		□ DNA sequencing	
		□ Analyzing gene expression	
		□ Determining gene function	
		□ Stem cells	
		□ Practical applications of DNA technology: medical applications, human gene therapy, pharmaceuticals, forensic evidence, environmental cleanup, agriculture	
		□ Recombinant DNA and Biotechnology (BIO) □ Safety and ethics of DNA technology	
□ **1C. Transmission of heritable information from generation to generation and the processes that increase genetic diversity**	□ Mendelian Concepts (BIO)	□ Phenotype and genotype	
		□ Gene	
		□ Locus	
		□ Allele: single and multiple	
		□ Homozygosity and heterozygosity	
		□ Wild-type	
		□ Recessiveness	
		□ Complete dominance	
		□ Co-dominance	
		□ Incomplete dominance, leakage, penetrance, expressivity	
		□ Hybridization: viability	
		□ Gene pool	
	□ Meiosis and Other Factors Affecting Genetic Variability (BIO)	□ Significance of meiosis	
		□ Important differences between meiosis and mitosis	
		□ Segregation of genes	□ Independent assortment □ Linkage □ Recombination □ Single crossovers □ Double crossovers □ Synaptonemal complex □ Tetrad □ Sex-linked characteristics □ Very few genes on Y chromosome □ Sex determination □ Cytoplasmic/extranuclear inheritance
		□ Mutation	□ General concept of mutation – error in DNA sequence □ Types of mutations: random, translation error, transcription error, base substitution, inversion, addition, deletion, translocation, mispairing □ Advantageous vs. deleterious mutation □ Inborn errors of metabolism □ Relationship of mutagens to carcinogens
	□ Analytic Methods (BIO)	□ Genetic drift	
		□ Synapsis or crossing-over mechanism for increasing genetic diversity	
		□ Hardy-Weinberg Principle	
		□ Testcross (Backcross; concepts of parental, F1, and F2 generations)	
		□ Gene mapping: crossover frequencies	
		□ Biometry: statistical methods	
	□ Evolution (BIO	□ Natural selection	□ Fitness concept □ Selection by differential reproduction □ Concepts of natural and group selection □ Evolutionary success as increase in percent representation in the gene pool of the next generation
		□ Speciation	□ Polymorphism □ Adaptation and specialization □ Inbreeding □ Outbreeding □ Bottlenecks
		□ Evolutionary time as measured by gradual random changes in genome	
□ **1D. Principles of bioenergetics and fuel molecule metabolism**	□ Principles of Bioenergetics (BC, GC)	□ Bioenergetics/ thermodynamics	□ Free energy/Keq □ Equilibrium constant □ Relationship of the equilibrium constant and $\Delta G°$ □ Concentration □ Le Châtelier's Principle □ Endothermic/exothermic reactions □ Free energy: G □ Spontaneous reactions and $\Delta G°$
		□ Phosphoryl group transfers and ATP	□ ATP hydrolysis $\Delta G << 0$ □ ATP group transfers
		□ Biological oxidation-reduction	□ Half-reactions □ Soluble electron carriers □ Flavoproteins
	□ Carbohydrates (BC, OC)	□ Description	□ Nomenclature and classification, common names □ Absolute configuration □ Cyclic structure and conformations of hexoses □ Epimers and anomers
		□ Hydrolysis of the glycoside linkage	
		□ Monosaccharides	
		□ Disaccharides	
		□ Polysaccharides	

	□ Glycolysis, Gluconeogenesis, and the Pentose Phosphate Pathway (BIO, BC)	□ Glycolysis (aerobic), substrates and products	□ Feeder pathways: glycogen, starch metabolism
		□ Fermentation (anaerobic glycolysis)	
		□ Gluconeogenesis (BC)	
		□ Pentose phosphate pathway (BC)	
		□ Net molecular and energetic results of respiration processes	
	□ Principles of Metabolic Regulation (BC)	□ Regulation of metabolic pathways (BIO, BC)	□ Maintenance of a dynamic steady state
		□ Regulation of glycolysis and gluconeogenesis	
		□ Metabolism of glycogen	
		□ Regulation of glycogen synthesis and breakdown	□ Allosteric and hormonal control
		□ Analysis of metabolic control	
	□ Citric Acid Cycle (BIO, BC)	□ Acetyl-CoA production (BC)	
		□ Reactions of the cycle, substrates and products	
		□ Regulation of the cycle	
		□ Net molecular and energetic results of respiration processes	
	□ Metabolism of Fatty Acids and Proteins (BIO, BC)	□ Description of fatty acids (BC)	
		□ Digestion, mobilization, and transport of fats	
		□ Oxidation of fatty acids	□ Saturated fats □ Unsaturated fats
		□ Ketone bodies (BC)	
		□ Anabolism of fats (BIO)	
		□ Non-template synthesis: biosynthesis of lipids and polysaccharides (BIO)	
		□ Metabolism of proteins (BIO)	
	□ Oxidative Phosphorylation (BIO, BC)	□ Electron transport chain and oxidative phosphorylation, substrates and products, general features of the pathway	
		□ Electron transfer in mitochondria	□ NADH, NADPH □ Flavoproteins □ Cytochromes
		□ ATP synthase, chemiosmotic coupling	□ Proton motive force
		□ Net molecular and energetic results of respiration processes	
		□ Regulation of oxidative phosphorylation	
		□ Mitochondria, apoptosis, oxidative stress (BC)	
	□ Hormonal Regulation and Integration of Metabolism (BC)	□ Higher level integration of hormone structure and function	
		□ Tissue specific metabolism	
		□ Hormonal regulation of fuel metabolism	
		□ Obesity and regulation of body mass	
□ Foundational Concept 2: Highly-organized assemblies of molecules, cells, and organs interact to carry out the functions of living organisms.			
□ **2A. Assemblies of molecules, cells, and groups of cells within single cellular and multicellular organisms**	□ Plasma Membrane (BIO, BC)	□ General function in cell containment	
		□ Composition of membranes	□ Lipid components (BIO, BC, OC) □ Phospholipids (and phosphatids) □ Steroids □ Waxes □ Protein components □ Fluid mosaic model
		□ Membrane dynamics	
		□ Solute transport across membranes	□ Thermodynamic considerations □ Colligative properties; osmotic pressure (GC) □ Osmosis □ Passive transport □ Active transport □ Sodium/potassium pump
		□ Membrane channels	
		□ Membrane potential	
		□ Membrane receptors	
		□ Exocytosis and endocytosis	
		□ Intercellular junctions (BIO)	□ Gap junctions □ Tight junctions □ Desmosomes
	□ Membrane-Bound Organelles and Defining Characteristics of Eukaryotic Cells (BIO)	□ Defining characteristics of eukaryotic cells: membrane bound nucleus, presence of organelles, mitotic division	
		□ Nucleus	□ Compartmentalization, storage of genetic information □ Nucleolus: location and function □ Nuclear envelope, nuclear pores
		□ Mitochondria	□ Site of ATP production □ Inner and outer membrane structure (BIO, BC) □ Self-replication
		□ Lysosomes: membrane-bound vesicles containing hydrolytic enzymes	
		□ Endoplasmic reticulum	□ Rough and smooth components □ Rough endoplasmic reticulum site of ribosomes □ Double membrane structure □ Role in membrane biosynthesis □ Role in biosynthesis of secreted proteins
		□ Golgi apparatus: general structure and role in packaging and secretion	
		□ Peroxisomes: organelles that collect peroxides	
	□ Cytoskeleton (BIO)	□ General function in cell support and movement	
		□ Microfilaments: composition and role in cleavage and contractility	
		□ Microtubules: composition and role in support and transport	
		□ Intermediate filaments, role in support	
		□ Composition and function of cilia and flagella	
		□ Centrioles, microtubule organizing centers	
	□ Tissues Formed From Eukaryotic Cells (BIO)	□ Epithelial cells	
		□ Connective tissue cells	

□ 2B. The structure, growth, physiology, and genetics of prokaryotes and viruses	□ Cell Theory (BIO)	□ History and development	
		□ Impact on biology	
	□ Classification and Structure of Prokaryotic Cells (BIO)	□ Prokaryotic domains	□ Archaea □ Bacteria
		□ Major classifications of bacteria by shape	□ Bacilli (rod-shaped) □ Spirilli (spiral-shaped) □ Cocci (spherical)
		□ Lack of nuclear membrane and mitotic apparatus	
		□ Lack of typical eukaryotic organelles	
		□ Presence of cell wall in bacteria	
		□ Flagellar propulsion, mechanism	
	□ Growth and Physiology of Prokaryotic Cells (BIO)	□ Reproduction by fission	
		□ High degree of genetic adaptability, acquisition of antibiotic resistance	
		□ Exponential growth	
		□ Existence of anaerobic and aerobic variants	
		□ Parasitic and symbiotic	
		□ Chemotaxis	
	□ Genetics of Prokaryotic Cells (BIO)	□ Existence of plasmids, extragenomic DNA	
		□ Transformation: incorporation into bacterial genome of DNA fragments from external medium	
		□ Conjugation	
		□ Transposons (also present in eukaryotic cells)	
	□ Virus Structure (BIO)	□ General structural characteristics (nucleic acid and protein, enveloped and nonenveloped)	
		□ Lack organelles and nucleus	
		□ Structural aspects of typical bacteriophage	
		□ Genomic content – RNA or DNA	
		□ Size relative to bacteria and eukaryotic cells	
	□ Viral Life Cycle (BIO)	□ Self replicating biological units that must reproduce within specific host cell	
		□ Generalized phage and animal virus life cycles	□ Attachment to host, penetration of cell membrane or cell wall, and entry of viral genetic material □ Use of host synthetic mechanism to replicate viral components □ Self-assembly and release of new viral particles
		□ Transduction: transfer of genetic material by viruses	
		□ Retrovirus life cycle: integration into host DNA, reverse transcriptase, HIV	
		□ Prions and viroids: subviral particles	
□ 2C. Processes of cell division, differentiation, and specialization	□ Mitosis (BIO)	□ Mitotic process: prophase, metaphase, anaphase, telophase, interphase	
		□ Mitotic structures	□ Centrioles, asters, spindles □ Chromatids, centromeres, kinetochores □ Nuclear membrane breakdown and reorganization □ Mechanisms of chromosome movement
		□ Phases of cell cycle: G0, G1, S, G2, M	
		□ Growth arrest	
		□ Control of cell cycle	
		□ Loss of cell cycle controls in cancer cells	
	□ Biosignalling (BC)	□ Oncogenes, apoptosis	
	□ Reproductive System (BIO)	□ Gametogenesis by meiosis	
		□ Ovum and sperm	□ Differences in formation □ Differences in morphology □ Relative contribution to next generation
		□ Reproductive sequence: fertilization; implantation; development; birth	

	□ Embryogenesis (BIO)	□ Stages of early development (order and general features of each)	□ Fertilization
			□ Cleavage
			□ Blastula formation
			□ Gastrulation
			  □ First cell movements
			  □ Formation of primary germ layers (endoderm, mesoderm, ectoderm)
			□ Neurulation

		□ Major structures arising out of primary germ layers	
		□ Neural crest	
		□ Environment–gene interaction in development	
	□ Mechanisms of Development (BIO)	□ Cell specialization	□ Determination □ Differentiation □ Tissue types
		□ Cell–cell communication in development	
		□ Cell migration	
		□ Pluripotency: stem cells	
		□ Gene regulation in development	
		□ Programmed cell death	
		□ Existence of regenerative capacity in various species	
		□ Senescence and aging	
□ Foundational Concept 3: Complex systems of tissues and organs sense the internal and external environments of multicellular organisms, and through integrated functioning, maintain a stable internal environment within an ever-changing external environment.			
□ 3A. Structure and functions of the nervous and endocrine systems and ways in which these systems coordinate the organ systems	□ Nervous System: Structure and Function (BIO)	□ Major Functions	□ High level control and integration of body systems □ Adaptive capability to external influences
		□ Organization of vertebrate nervous system	
		□ Sensor and effector neurons	
		□ Sympathetic and parasympathetic nervous systems: antagonistic control	
		□ Reflexes	□ Feedback loop, reflex arc □ Role of spinal cord and supraspinal circuits
		□ Integration with endocrine system: feedback control	
	□ Nerve Cell (BIO)	□ Cell body: site of nucleus, organelles	
		□ Dendrites: branched extensions of cell body	
		□ Axon: structure and function	
		□ Myelin sheath, Schwann cells, insulation of axon	
		□ Nodes of Ranvier: propagation of nerve impulse along axon	
		□ Synapse: site of impulse propagation between cells	
		□ Synaptic activity: transmitter molecules	
		□ Resting potential: electrochemical gradient	

		□ Action potential	□ Threshold, all-or-none □ Sodium/potassium pump
		□ Excitatory and inhibitory nerve fibers: summation, frequency of firing	
		□ Glial cells, neuroglia	
	□ Electrochemistry (GC)	□ Concentration cell: direction of electron flow, Nernst equation	
	□ Biosignalling (BC)	□ Gated ion channels	□ Voltage gated □ Ligand gated
		□ Receptor enzymes	
		□ G protein-coupled receptors	
	□ Lipids (BC, OC)	□ Description; structure	□ Steroids □ Terpenes and terpenoids
	□ Endocrine System: Hormones and Their Sources (BIO)	□ Function of endocrine system: specific chemical control at cell, tissue, and organ level	
		□ Definitions of endocrine gland, hormone	
		□ Major endocrine glands: names, locations, products	
		□ Major types of hormones	
		□ Neuroendrocrinology — relation between neurons and hormonal systems	
	□ Endocrine System: Mechanisms of Hormone Action (BIO)	□ Cellular mechanisms of hormone action	
		□ Transport of hormones: blood supply	
		□ Specificity of hormones: target tissue	
		□ Integration with nervous system: feedback control	
		□ Regulation by second messengers	
□ **3B. Structure and integrative functions of the main organ systems**	□ Respiratory System (BIO)	□ General function	□ Gas exchange, thermoregulation □ Protection against disease: particulate matter
		□ Structure of lungs and alveoli	
		□ Breathing mechanisms	□ Diaphragm, rib cage, differential pressure □ Resiliency and surface tension effects
		□ Thermoregulation: nasal and tracheal capillary beds; evaporation, panting	
		□ Particulate filtration: nasal hairs, mucus/cilia system in lungs	
		□ Alveolar gas exchange	□ Diffusion, differential partial pressure □ Henry's Law (GC)
		□ pH control	
		□ Regulation by nervous control	□ CO2 sensitivity
	□ Circulatory System (BIO)	□ Functions: circulation of oxygen, nutrients, hormones, ions and fluids, removal of metabolic waste	
		□ Role in thermoregulation	
		□ Four-chambered heart: structure and function	
		□ Endothelial cells	
		□ Systolic and diastolic pressure	
		□ Pulmonary and systemic circulation	
		□ Arterial and venous systems (arteries, arterioles, venules, veins)	□ Structural and functional differences □ Pressure and flow characteristics
		□ Capillary beds	□ Mechanisms of gas and solute exchange □ Mechanism of heat exchange □ Source of peripheral resistance
		□ Composition of blood	□ Plasma, chemicals, blood cells □ Erythrocyte production and destruction; spleen, bone marrow □ Regulation of plasma volume
		□ Coagulation, clotting mechanisms	
		□ Oxygen transport by blood	□ Hemoglobin, haematocrit □ Oxygen content □ Oxygen affinity
		□ Carbon dioxide transport and level in blood	
		□ Nervous and endocrine control	
	□ Lymphatic System (BIO)	□ Structure of lymphatic system	
		□ Major functions	□ Equalization of fluid distribution □ Transport of proteins and large glycerides □ Production of lymphocytes involved in immune reactions □ Return of materials to the blood
	□ Immune System (BIO)	□ Innate (non-specific) vs. adaptive (specific) immunity	
		□ Adaptive immune system cells	□ T-lymphocytes □ B-lymphocytes
		□ Innate immune system cells	□ Macrophages □ Phagocytes
		□ Tissues	□ Bone marrow □ Spleen □ Thymus □ Lymph nodes
		□ Concept of antigen and antibody	
		□ Antigen presentation	
		□ Clonal selection	
		□ Antigen-antibody recognition	
		□ Structure of antibody molecule	
		□ Recognition of self vs. non-self, autoimmune diseases	
		□ Major histocompatibility complex	
	□ Digestive System (BIO)	□ Ingestion	□ Saliva as lubrication and source of enzymes □ Ingestion; esophagus, transport function
		□ Stomach	□ Storage and churning of food □ Low pH, gastric juice, mucal protection against self-destruction □ Production of digestive enzymes, site of digestion □ Structure (gross)
		□ Liver	□ Structural relationship of liver within gastrointestinal system □ Production of bile □ Role in blood glucose regulation, detoxification
		□ Bile	□ Storage in gall bladder □ Function
		□ Pancreas	□ Production of enzymes □ Transport of enzymes to small intestine

		□ Small Intestine	□ Absorption of food molecules and water □ Function and structure of villi □ Production of enzymes, site of digestion □ Neutralization of stomach acid □ Structure (anatomic subdivisions)
		□ Large Intestine	□ Absorption of water □ Bacterial flora □ Structure (gross)
		□ Rectum: storage and elimination of waste, feces	
		□ Muscular control	□ Peristalsis
		□ Endocrine control	□ Hormones □ Target tissues
		□ Nervous control: the enteric nervous system	
	□ Excretory System (BIO)	□ Roles in homeostasis	□ Blood pressure □ Osmoregulation □ Acid-base balance □ Removal of soluble nitrogenous waste
		□ Kidney structure	□ Cortex □ Medulla
		□ Nephron structure	□ Glomerulus □ Bowman's capsule □ Proximal tubule □ Loop of Henle □ Distal tubule □ Collecting duct
		□ Formation of urine	□ Glomerular filtration □ Secretion and reabsorption of solutes □ Concentration of urine □ Counter-current multiplier mechanism
		□ Storage and elimination: ureter, bladder, urethra	
		□ Osmoregulation: capillary reabsorption of H2O, amino acids, glucose, ions	
		□ Muscular control: sphincter muscle	
	□ Reproductive System (BIO)	□ Male and female reproductive structures and their functions	□ Gonads □ Genitalia □ Differences between male and female structures
		□ Hormonal control of reproduction	□ Male and female sexual development □ Female reproductive cycle □ Pregnancy, parturition, lactation □ Integration with nervous control
	□ Muscle System (BIO)	□ Important functions	□ Support: mobility □ Peripheral circulatory assistance □ Thermoregulation (shivering reflex)
		□ Structure of three basic muscle types: striated, smooth, cardiac	
		□ Muscle structure and control of contraction	□ T-tubule system □ Contractile apparatus □ Sarcoplasmic reticulum □ Fiber type □ Contractile velocity of different muscle types
		□ Regulation of cardiac muscle contraction	
		□ Oxygen debt: fatigue	
		□ Nervous control	□ Motor neurons □ Neuromuscular junction, motor end plates □ Sympathetic and parasympathetic innervation □ Voluntary and involuntary muscles
	□ Specialized Cell - Muscle Cell (BIO)	□ Structural characteristics of striated, smooth, and cardiac muscle	
		□ Abundant mitochondria in red muscle cells: ATP source	
		□ Organization of contractile elements: actin and myosin filaments, crossbridges, sliding filament model	
		□ Sarcomeres: "I" and "A" bands, "M" and "Z" lines, "H" zone	
		□ Presence of troponin and tropomyosin	
		□ Calcium regulation of contraction	
	□ Skeletal System (BIO)	□ Functions	□ Structural rigidity and support □ Calcium storage □ Physical protection
		□ Skeletal structure	□ Specialization of bone types, structures □ Joint structures □ Endoskeleton vs. exoskeleton
		□ Bone structure	□ Calcium/protein matrix □ Cellular composition of bone
		□ Cartilage: structure and function	
		□ Ligaments, tendons	
		□ Endocrine control	
	□ Skin System (BIO)	□ Structure	□ Layer differentiation, cell types □ Relative impermeability to water
		□ Functions in homeostasis and osmoregulation	
		□ Functions in thermoregulation	□ Hair, erectile musculature □ Fat layer for insulation □ Sweat glands, location in dermis □ Vasoconstriction and vasodilation in surface capillaries
		□ Physical protection	□ Nails, calluses, hair □ Protection against abrasion, disease organisms
		□ Hormonal control: sweating, vasodilation, and vasoconstriction	

□ Section 2: Chemical and Physical Foundations of Biological Systems			
□ Foundational Concept 4: Complex living organisms transport materials, sense their environment, process signals, and respond to changes using processes understood in terms of physical principles.			
□ **4A. Translational motion, forces, work, energy, and equilibrium in living systems**	□ Translational Motion (PHY)	□ Units and dimensions	
		□ Vectors, components	
		□ Vector addition	
		□ Speed, velocity (average and instantaneous)	
		□ Acceleration	
	□ Force (PHY)	□ Newton's First Law, inertia	
		□ Newton's Second Law (F = ma)	
		□ Newton's Third Law, forces equal and opposite	
		□ Friction, static and kinetic	
		□ Center of mass	
	□ Equilibrium (PHY)	□ Vector analysis of forces acting on a point object	
		□ Torques, lever arms	
	□ Work (PHY)	□ Work done by a constant force: $W = Fd\cos\theta$	
		□ Mechanical advantage	
		□ Work Kinetic Energy Theorem	
		□ Conservative forces	
	□ Energy of Point Object Systems (PHY)	□ Kinetic Energy: $KE = \frac{1}{2}mv^2$; units	
		□ Potential Energy	□ $PE = mgh$ (gravitational, local) □ $PE = \frac{1}{2}kx^2$ (spring)
		□ Conservation of energy	
		□ Power, units	
	□ Periodic Motion (PHY	□ Amplitude, frequency, phase	
		□ Transverse and longitudinal waves: wavelength and propagation speed	
□ **4B. Importance of fluids for the circulation of blood, gas movement, and gas exchange**	□ Fluids (PHY)	□ Density, specific gravity	
		□ Buoyancy, Archimedes' Principle	
		□ Hydrostatic pressure	□ Pascal's Law □ Hydrostatic pressure; $P = \rho gh$ (pressure vs. depth)
		□ Viscosity: Poiseuille Flow	
		□ Continuity equation ($A \cdot v$ = constant)	
		□ Concept of turbulence at high velocities	
		□ Surface tension	
		□ Bernoulli's equation	
		□ Venturi effect, pitot tube	
	□ Circulatory System (BIO)	□ Arterial and venous systems; pressure and flow characteristics	
	□ Gas Phase (GC, PHY)	□ Absolute temperature, (K) Kelvin Scale	
		□ Pressure, simple mercury barometer	
		□ Molar volume at 0°C and 1 atm = 22.4 L/mol	
		□ Ideal gas	□ Definition □ Ideal Gas Law: $PV = nRT$ □ Boyle's Law: PV = constant □ Charles' Law: V/T = constant □ Avogadro's Law: V/n = constant
		□ Kinetic Molecular Theory of Gases	□ Heat capacity at constant volume and at constant pressure (PHY) □ Boltzmann's Constant (PHY)
		□ Deviation of real gas behavior from Ideal Gas Law	□ Qualitative □ Quantitative (Van der Waals' Equation)
		□ Partial pressure, mole fraction	
		□ Dalton's Law relating partial pressure to composition	
□ **4C. Electrochemistry and electrical circuits and their elements**	□ Electrostatics (PHY)	□ Charge, conductors, charge conservation	
		□ Insulators	
		□ Coulomb's Law	
		□ Electric field E	□ Field lines □ Field due to charge distribution
		□ Electrostatic energy, electric potential at a point in space	
	□ Circuit Elements (PHY)	□ Current $I = \Delta Q/\Delta t$, sign conventions, units	
		□ Electromotive force, voltage	
		□ Resistance	□ Ohm's Law: $I = V/R$ □ Resistors in series □ Resistors in parallel □ Resistivity: $\rho = R \bullet A / L$
		□ Capacitance	□ Parallel plate capacitor □ Energy of charged capacitor □ Capacitors in series □ Capacitors in parallel □ Dielectrics
		□ Conductivity	○ Metallic ○ Electrolytic
		□ Meters	
	□ Magnetism (PHY)	□ Definition of magnetic field	
		□ Motion of charged particles in magnetic fields; Lorentz force	
	□ Electrochemistry (GC)	□ Electrolytic cell	□ Electrolysis □ Anode, cathode □ Electrolyte □ Faraday's Law relating amount of elements deposited (or gas liberated) at an electrode to current □ Electron flow; oxidation, and reduction at the electrodes
		□ Galvanic or Voltaic cells	□ Half-reactions □ Reduction potentials; cell potential □ Direction of electron flow
		□ Concentration cell	

		□ Batteries	□ Electromotive force, Voltage □ Lead-storage batteries □ Nickel-cadmium batteries
	□ Specialized Cell - Nerve Cell (BIO)	□ Myelin sheath, Schwann cells, insulation of axon	
		□ Nodes of Ranvier: propagation of nerve impulse along axon	
□ **4D. How light and sound interact with matter**	□ Sound (PHY)	□ Production of sound	
		□ Relative speed of sound in solids, liquids, and gases	
		□ Intensity of sound, decibel units, log scale	
		□ Attenuation (Damping)	
		□ Doppler Effect: moving sound source or observer, reflection of sound from a moving object	
		□ Pitch	
		□ Resonance in pipes and strings	
		□ Ultrasound	
		□ Shock waves	
	□ Light, Electromagnetic Radiation (PHY)	□ Concept of Interference; Young Double-slit Experiment	
		□ Thin films, diffraction grating, single-slit diffraction	
		□ Other diffraction phenomena, X-ray diffraction	
		□ Polarization of light: linear and circular	
		□ Properties of electromagnetic radiation	□ Velocity equals constant c, in vacuo □ Electromagnetic radiation consists of perpendicularly oscillating electric and magnetic fields; direction of propagation is perpendicular to both
		□ Classification of electromagnetic spectrum, photon energy $E = hf$	
		□ Visual spectrum, color	
	□ Molecular Structure and Absorption Spectra (OC)	□ Infrared region	□ Intramolecular vibrations and rotations □ Recognizing common characteristic group absorptions, fingerprint region
		□ Visible region (GC)	□ Absorption in visible region gives complementary color (e.g., carotene) □ Effect of structural changes on absorption (e.g., indicators)
		□ Ultraviolet region	□ π-Electron and non-bonding electron transitions □ Conjugated systems
		□ NMR spectroscopy	□ Protons in a magnetic field; equivalent protons □ Spin-spin splitting
	□ Geometrical Optics (PHY)	□ Reflection from plane surface: angle of incidence equals angle of reflection	
		□ Refraction, refractive index n; Snell's law: $n1 \sin \theta 1 = n2 \sin \theta 2$	
		□ Dispersion, change of index of refraction with wavelength	
		□ Conditions for total internal reflection	
		□ Spherical mirrors	□ Center of curvature □ Focal length □ Real and virtual images
		□ Thin lenses	□ Converging and diverging lenses □ Use of formula $1/p + 1/q = 1/f$, with sign conventions □ Lens strength, diopters
		□ Combination of lenses	
		□ Lens aberration	
		□ Optical Instruments, including the human eye	
□ **4E. Atoms, nuclear decay, electronic structure, and atomic chemical behavior**	□ Atomic Nucleus (PHY, GC)	□ Atomic number, atomic weight	
		□ Neutrons, protons, isotopes	
		□ Nuclear forces, binding energy	
		□ Radioactive decay	□ α, β, γ decay □ Half-life, exponential decay, semi-log plots
		□ Mass spectrometer	
	□ Electronic Structure (PHY, GC)	□ Orbital structure of hydrogen atom, principal quantum number n, number of electrons per orbital (GC)	
		□ Ground state, excited states	
		□ Absorption and emission line spectra	
		□ Use of Pauli Exclusion Principle	
		□ Paramagnetism and diamagnetism	
		□ Conventional notation for electronic structure (GC)	
		□ Bohr atom	
		□ Heisenberg Uncertainty Principle	
		□ Effective nuclear charge (GC)	
		□ Photoelectric effect	
	□ The Periodic Table - Classification of Elements into Groups by Electronic Structure (GC)	□ Alkali metals	
		□ Alkaline earth metals: their chemical characteristics	
		□ Halogens: their chemical characteristics	
		□ Noble gases: their physical and chemical characteristics	
		□ Transition metals	
		□ Representative elements	
		□ Metals and non-metals	
		□ Oxygen group	
	□ The Periodic Table - Variations of Chemical Properties with Group and Row (GC)	□ Valence electrons	
		□ First and second ionization energy	□ Definition □ Prediction from electronic structure for elements in different groups or rows
		□ Electron affinity	□ Definition □ Variation with group and row
		□ Electronegativity	□ Definition □ Comparative values for some representative elements and important groups
		□ Electron shells and the sizes of atoms	
		□ Electron shells and the sizes of ions	
	□ Stoichiometry (GC)	□ Molecular weight	
		□ Empirical versus molecular formula	
		□ Metric units commonly used in the context of chemistry	

		□ Description of composition by percent mass	
		□ Mole concept, Avogadro's number NA	
		□ Definition of density	
		□ Oxidation number	□ Common oxidizing and reducing agents □ Disproportionation reactions
		□ Description of reactions by chemical equations	□ Conventions for writing chemical equations □ Balancing equations, including redox equations □ Limiting reactants □ Theoretical yields
□ Foundational Concept 5: The principles that govern chemical interactions and reactions form the basis for a broader understanding of the molecular dynamics of living systems.			
□ **5A. Unique nature of water and its solutions**	□ Acid/Base Equilibria (GC, BC)	□ Brønsted-Lowry definition of acid, base	
		□ Ionization of water	□ K_w, its approximate value ($K_w = [H^+][OH^-] = 10^{-14}$ at 25°C, 1 atm) □ Definition of pH: pH of pure water
		□ Conjugate acids and bases (e.g., NH_4^+ and NH_3)	
		□ Strong acids and bases (e.g., nitric, sulfuric)	
		□ Weak acids and bases (e.g., acetic, benzoic)	□ Dissociation of weak acids and bases with or without added salt □ Hydrolysis of salts of weak acids or bases □ Calculation of pH of solutions of salts of weak acids or bases
		□ Equilibrium constants K_a and K_b: pK_a, pK_b	
		□ Buffers	□ Definition and concepts (common buffer systems) □ Influence on titration curves
	□ Ions in Solutions (GC, BC)	□ Anion, cation: common names, formulas and charges for familiar ions (e.g., NH_4^+ ammonium, PO_4^{3-} phosphate, SO_4^{2-} sulfate)	
		□ Hydration, the hydronium ion	
	□ Solubility (GC)	□ Units of concentration (e.g., molarity)	
		□ Solubility product constant; the equilibrium expression K_{sp}	
		□ Common-ion effect, its use in laboratory separations	□ Complex ion formation □ Complex ions and solubility □ Solubility and pH
	□ Titration (GC	□ Indicators	
		□ Neutralization	
		□ Interpretation of the titration curves	
		□ Redox titration	
□ **5B. Nature of molecules and intermolecular interactions**	□ Covalent Bond (GC)	□ Lewis Electron Dot formulas	□ Resonance structures □ Formal charge □ Lewis acids and bases
		□ Partial ionic character	□ Role of electronegativity in determining charge distribution □ Dipole Moment
		□ σ and π bonds	□ Hybrid orbitals: sp^3, sp^2, sp and respective geometries □ Valence shell electron pair repulsion and the prediction of shapes of molecules (e.g., NH_3, H_2O, CO_2) □ Structural formulas for molecules involving H, C, N, O, F, S, P, Si, Cl □ Delocalized electrons and resonance in ions and molecules
		□ Multiple bonding	□ Effect on bond length and bond energies □ Rigidity in molecular structure

		□ Stereochemistry of covalently bonded molecules (OC)	□ Isomers
			  □ Structural isomers
			  □ Stereoisomers (e.g., diastereomers, enantiomers, cis/trans isomers)
			  □ Conformational isomers
			□ Polarization of light, specific rotation
			□ Absolute and relative configuration
			  □ Conventions for writing R and S forms
			  □ Conventions for writing E and Z forms

	□ Liquid Phase - Intermolecular Forces (GC)	□ Hydrogen bonding	
		□ Dipole Interactions	
		□ Van der Waals' Forces (London dispersion forces)	
□ **5C. Separation and purification methods**	□ Separations and Purifications (OC, BC)	□ Extraction: distribution of solute between two immiscible solvents	
		□ Distillation	

		□ Chromatography: Basic principles involved in separation process	□ Column chromatography
			  □ Gas-liquid chromatography
			  □ High pressure liquid chromatography
			□ Paper chromatography
			□ Thin-layer chromatography

		□ Separation and purification of peptides and proteins (BC)	□ Electrophoresis
			□ Quantitative analysis
			□ Chromatography
			  □ Size-exclusion
			  □ Ion-exchange
			  □ Affinity

		□ Racemic mixtures, separation of enantiomers (OC)	
□ **5D. Structure, function, and reactivity of biologically-relevant molecules**	□ Nucleotides and Nucleic Acids (BC, BIO)	□ Nucleotides and nucleosides: composition	□ Sugar phosphate backbone □ Pyrimidine, purine residues
		□ Deoxyribonucleic acid: DNA; double helix	
		□ Chemistry (BC)	
		□ Other functions (BC)	

	□ Amino Acids, Peptides, Proteins (OC, BC)	□ Amino acids: description	□ Absolute configuration at the α position
			□ Dipolar ions
			□ Classification
			  □ Acidic or basic
			  □ Hydrophilic or hydrophobic
			□ Synthesis of α-amino acids (OC)
			  □ Strecker Synthesis
			  □ Gabriel Synthesis

		□ Peptides and proteins: reactions	□ Sulfur linkage for cysteine and cysteine □ Peptide linkage: polypeptides and proteins □ Hydrolysis (BC)
		□ General Principles	□ Primary structure of proteins □ Secondary structure of proteins □ Tertiary structure of proteins □ Isoelectric point
	□ The Three-Dimensional Protein Structure (BC)	□ Conformational stability	□ Hydrophobic interactions □ Solvation layer (entropy)
		□ Quaternary structure	
		□ Denaturing and Folding	

	□ Non-Enzymatic Protein Function (BC)	□ Binding	
		□ Immune system	
		□ Motor	

	□ Lipids (BC, OC)	□ Description, Types	□ Storage
			  □ Triacyl glycerols
			  □ Free fatty acids: saponification
			□ Structural
			  □ Phospholipids and phosphatides
			  □ Sphingolipids (BC)
			  □ Waxes
			□ Signals/cofactors
			  □ Fat-soluble vitamins
			  □ Steroids
			  □ Prostaglandins (BC)

	□ Carbohydrates (OC)	□ Description	□ Nomenclature and classification, common names □ Absolute configuration □ Cyclic structure and conformations of hexoses □ Epimers and anomers
		□ Hydrolysis of the glycoside linkage	
		□ Keto-enol tautomerism of monosaccharides	
		□ Disaccharides (BC)	
		□ Polysaccharides (BC)	
	□ Aldehydes and Ketones (OC)	□ Description	□ Nomenclature □ Physical properties

		□ Important reactions	□ Nucleophilic addition reactions at C=O bond
			  □ Acetal, hemiacetal
			  □ Imine, enamine
			  □ Hydride reagents
			  □ Cyanohydrin
			□ Oxidation of aldehydes
			□ Reactions at adjacent positions: enolate chemistry
			  □ Keto-enol tautomerism (α-racemization)
			  □ Aldol condensation, retro-aldol
			  □ Kinetic versus thermodynamic enolate

		□ General principles	□ Effect of substituents on reactivity of C=O; steric hindrance □ Acidity of α-H; carbanions
	□ Alcohols (OC)	□ Description	□ Nomenclature □ Physical properties (acidity, hydrogen bonding)
		□ Important reactions	□ Oxidation □ Substitution reactions: S_N1 or S_N2 □ Protection of alcohols □ Preparation of mesylates and tosylates
	□ Carboxylic Acids (OC)	□ Description	□ Nomenclature □ Physical properties

		□ Important reactions	□ Carboxyl group reactions
			  □ Amides (and lactam), esters (and lactone), anhydride formation
			  □ Reduction
			  □ Decarboxylation
			□ Reactions at 2-position, substitution

	□ Acid Derivatives (Anhydrides, Amides, Esters) (OC)	□ Description	□ Nomenclature □ Physical properties
		□ Important reactions	□ Nucleophilic substitution □ Transesterification □ Hydrolysis of amides
		□ General principles	□ Relative reactivity of acid derivatives □ Steric effects □ Electronic effects □ Strain (e.g., β-lactams)
	□ Phenols (OC, BC)	□ Oxidation and reduction (e.g., hydroquinones, ubiquinones): biological 2e– redox centers	
	□ Polycyclic/Heterocyclic AromaticCompoundOC,BC	□ Biological aromatic heterocycles	
□ 5E. Principles of chemical thermodynamics and kinetics	□ Enzymes (BC, BIO)	□ Classification by reaction type	
		□ Mechanism	□ Substrates and enzyme specificity □ Active site model □ Induced-fit model □ Cofactors, coenzymes, and vitamins
		□ Kinetics	□ General (catalysis) □ Michaelis-Menten □ Cooperativity □ Effects of local conditions on enzyme activity
		□ Inhibition	
		□ Regulatory enzymes	□ Allosteric □ Covalently modified
	□ Principles of Bioenergetics (BC)	□ Bioenergetics/ thermodynamics	□ Free energy/K_{eq} □ Concentration
		□ Phosphorylation/ATP	□ ATP hydrolysis $\Delta G << 0$ □ ATP group transfers
		□ Biological oxidation-reduction	□ Half-reactions □ Soluble electron carriers □ Flavoproteins
	□ Energy Changes in Chemical Reactions – Thermochemistry, Thermodynamics (GC, PHY)	□ Thermodynamic system – state function	
		□ Zeroth Law – concept of temperature	
		□ First Law – conservation of energy in thermodynamic processes	
		□ PV diagram: work done = area under or enclosed by curve (PHY)	
		□ Second Law – concept of entropy	□ Entropy as a measure of "disorder" □ Relative entropy for gas, liquid, and crystal states
		□ Measurement of heat changes (calorimetry), heat capacity, specific heat	
		□ Heat transfer – conduction, convection, radiation (PHY)	
		□ Endothermic/ exothermic reactions (GC)	□ Enthalpy, H, and standard heats of reaction and formation □ Hess' Law of Heat Summation
		□ Bond dissociation energy as related to heats of formation (GC)	
		□ Free energy: G (GC)	
		□ Spontaneous reactions and $\Delta G°$ (GC)	
		□ Coefficient of expansion (PHY)	
		□ Heat of fusion, heat of vaporization	
		□ Phase diagram: pressure and temperature	

	□ Rate Processes in Chemical Reactions - Kinetics and Equilibrium (GC)	□ Reaction rate	
		□ Dependence of reaction rate on concentration of reactants	□ Rate law, rate constant □ Reaction order
		□ Rate-determining step	
		□ Dependence of reaction rate upon temperature	□ Activation energy □ Activated complex or transition state □ Interpretation of energy profiles showing energies of reactants, products, activation energy, and ΔH for the reaction □ Use of the Arrhenius Equation
		□ Kinetic control versus thermodynamic control of a reaction	
		□ Catalysts	
		□ Equilibrium in reversible chemical reactions	□ Law of Mass Action □ Equilibrium Constant □ Application of Le Châtelier's Principle
		□ Relationship of the equilibrium constant and ΔG°	

□ Section 3: Psychological, Social, and Biological Foundations of Behavior			
□ Foundational Concept 6: Biological, psychological, and sociocultural factors influence the ways that individuals perceive, think about, and react to the world.			
□ **6A. Sensing the environment**	□ Sensory Processing (PSY, BIO)	□ Sensation	□ Threshold □ Weber's Law (PSY) □ Signal detection theory (PSY) □ Sensory adaptation □ Psychophysics
		□ Sensory receptors	□ Sensory pathways □ Types of sensory receptor
	□ Vision (PSY, BIO)	□ Structure and function of the eye	
		□ Visual processing	□ Visual pathways in the brain □ Parallel processing (PSY) □ Feature detection (PSY)
	□ Hearing (PSY, BIO)	□ Structure and function of the ear	
		□ Auditory processing (e.g., auditory pathways in the brain)	
		□ Sensory reception by hair cells	
	□ Other Senses (PSY, BIO)	□ Somatosensation (e.g., pain perception)	
		□ Taste (e.g., taste buds/chemoreceptors that detect specific chemicals)	
		□ Smell	□ Olfactory cells/chemoreceptors that detect specific chemicals □ Pheromones (BIO) □ Olfactory pathways in the brain (BIO)
		□ Kinesthetic sense (PSY)	
		□ Vestibular sense	
	□ Perception (PSY)	□ Bottom-up/Top-down processing	
		□ Perceptual organization (e.g., depth, form, motion, constancy)	
		□ Gestalt principles	
□ **6B. Making sense of the environment**	□ Attention (PSY)	□ Selective attention	
		□ Divided attention	
	□ Cognition (PSY)	□ Information-processing model	
		□ Cognitive development	□ Piaget's stages of cognitive development □ Cognitive changes in late adulthood □ Role of culture in cognitive development □ Influence of heredity and environment on cognitive development
		□ Biological factors that affect cognition (PSY, BIO)	
		□ Problem solving and decision making	□ Types of problem solving □ Barriers to effective problem solving □ Approaches to problem solving □ Heuristics and biases (e.g., overconfidence, belief perseverance)
		□ Intellectual functioning	□ Theories of intelligence □ Influence of heredity and environment on intelligence □ Variations in intellectual ability
	□ Consciousness (PSY)	□ States of consciousness	□ Alertness (PSY, BIO) □ Sleep □ Stages of sleep □ Sleep cycles and changes to sleep cycles □ Sleep and circadian rhythms (PSY, BIO) □ Dreaming □ Sleep-wake disorders □ Hypnosis and meditation
		□ Consciousness-altering drugs	□ Types of consciousness-altering drugs and their effects on the nervous system and behaviour □ Drug addiction and the reward pathway in the brain
	□ Memory (PSY)	□ Encoding	□ Process of encoding information □ Processes that aid in encoding memories
		□ Storage	□ Types of memory storage (e.g., sensory, working, long-term) □ Semantic networks and spreading activation
		□ Retrieval	□ Recall, recognition, and relearning □ Retrieval cues □ The role of emotion in retrieving memories (PSY, BIO) □ Processes that aid retrieval
		□ Forgetting	□ Aging and memory □ Memory dysfunctions (e.g., Alzheimer's disease, Korsakoff's syndrome) □ Decay □ Interference □ Memory construction and source monitoring
		□ Changes in synaptic connections underlie memory and learning (PSY, BIO)	□ Neural plasticity □ Memory and learning □ Long-term potentiation
	□ Language (PSY)	□ Theories of language development (e.g., learning, Nativist, Interactionist)	
		□ Influence of language on cognition	
		□ Brain areas that control language and speech (PSY, BIO)	
□ **6C. Responding to the world**	□ Emotion (PSY)	□ Three components of emotion (i.e., cognitive, physiological, behavioral)	
		□ Universal emotions (i.e., fear, anger, happiness, surprise, joy, disgust, and sadness)	
		□ Adaptive role of emotion	
		□ Theories of emotion	□ James-Lange theory □ Cannon-Bard theory □ Schachter-Singer theory

		□ The role of biological processes in perceiving emotion (PSY, BIO)	□ Brain regions involved in the generation and experience of emotion □ The role of the limbic system in emotion □ Emotion and the autonomic nervous system □ Physiological markers of emotion (signatures of emotion)
	□ Stress (PSY)	□ The nature of stress	□ Appraisal □ Different types of stressors (e.g., cataclysmic events, personal) □ Effects of stress on psychological functions
		□ Stress outcomes/response to stressors	□ Physiological (PSY, BIO) □ Emotional □ Behavioral
		□ Managing stress (e.g., exercise, relaxation, spirituality)	
□ Foundational Concept 7: Biological, psychological, and sociocultural factors influence behavior and behavior change.			
□ **7A. Individual influences on behavior**	□ Biological Bases of Behavior (PSY, BIO)	□ The nervous system	□ Neurons (e.g., the reflex arc) □ Neurotransmitters □ Structure and function of the peripheral nervous system □ Structure and function of the central nervous system □ The brain □ Forebrain □ Midbrain □ Hindbrain □ Lateralization of cortical functions □ Methods used in studying the brain □ The spinal cord
		□ Neuronal communication and its influence on behavior (PSY)	
		□ Influence of neurotransmitters on behavior (PSY)	
		□ The endocrine system	□ Components of the endocrine system □ Effects of the endocrine system on behaviour
		□ Behavioral genetics	□ Genes, temperament, and heredity □ Adaptive value of traits and behaviors □ Interaction between heredity and environmental influences
			□ Genes, temperament, and heredity □ Adaptive value of traits and behaviors □ Interaction between heredity and environmental influences
		□ Influence of genetic and environmental factors on the development of behaviors	□ Experience and behavior (PSY) □ Regulatory genes and behavior (BIO) □ Genetically based behavioral variation in natural populations
		□ Human physiological development (PSY)	□ Prenatal development □ Motor development □ Developmental changes in adolescence
	□ Personality (PSY)	□ Theories of personality	□ Psychoanalytic perspective □ Humanistic perspective □ Trait perspective □ Social cognitive perspective □ Biological perspective □ Behaviorist perspective
		□ Situational approach to explaining behavior	
	□ Psychological Disorders (PSY)	□ Understanding psychological disorders	□ Biomedical vs. biopsychosocial approaches □ Classifying psychological disorders □ Rates of psychological disorders
		□ Types of psychological disorders	□ Anxiety disorders □ Obsessive-compulsive disorder □ Trauma- and stressor-related disorders □ Somatic symptom and related disorders □ Bipolar and related disorders □ Depressive disorders □ Schizophrenia □ Dissociative disorders □ Personality disorders
		□ Biological bases of nervous system disorders (PSY, BIO)	□ Schizophrenia □ Depression □ Alzheimer's disease □ Parkinson's disease □ Stem cell-based therapy to regenerate neurons in the central nervous system (BIO)
	□ Motivation (PSY)	□ Factors that influence motivation	□ Instinct □ Arousal □ Drives (e.g., negative feedback systems) (PSY, BIO) □ Needs
		□ Theories that explain how motivation affects human behavior	□ Drive reduction theory □ Incentive theory □ Other theories (e.g., cognitive, need-based)
		□ Biological and sociocultural motivators that regulate behavior (e.g., hunger, sex drive, substance addiction)	
	□ Attitudes (PSY)	□ Components of attitudes (i.e., cognitive, affective, and behavioral)	
		□ The link between attitudes and behavior	□ Processes by which behavior influences attitudes (e.g., foot-in-the door phenomenon, role-playing effects) □ Processes by which attitudes influence behaviour □ Cognitive dissonance theory
□ **7B. Social processes that influence human behavior**	□ How the Presence of Others Affects Individual Behavior (PSY)	□ Social facilitation	
		□ Deindividuation	
		□ Bystander effect	
		□ Social loafing	
		□ Social control (SOC)	
		□ Peer pressure (PSY, SOC)	
		□ Conformity (PSY, SOC)	
		□ Obedience (PSY, SOC)	
	□ Group Decision-making Processes (PSY, SOC)	□ Group polarization (PSY)	
		□ Groupthink	
	□ Normative and Non-normative Behavior (SOC)	□ Social norms (PSY, SOC)	□ Sanctions (SOC) □ Folkways, mores, and taboos (SOC) □ Anomie (SOC)
		□ Deviance	□ Perspectives on deviance (e.g., differential association, labeling theory, strain theory)
		□ Aspects of collective behavior (e.g., fads, mass hysteria, riots)	
	□ Socialization (PSY, SOC)	□ Agents of socialization (e.g., the family, mass media, peers, workplace)	
□ **7C. Attitude and behavior change**	□ Associative Learning (PSY)	□ Classical conditioning (PSY, BIO)	□ Neutral, conditioned, and unconditioned stimuli □ Conditioned and unconditioned response □ Processes: acquisition, extinction, spontaneous recovery, generalization, discrimination

		□ Operant conditioning (PSY, BIO)	□ Processes of shaping and extinction □ Types of reinforcement: positive, negative, primary, conditional □ Reinforcement schedules: fixed-ratio, variable-ratio, fixed-interval, variable-interval □ Punishment □ Escape and avoidance learning
		□ The role of cognitive processes in associative learning	
		□ Biological processes that affect associative learning (e.g., biological predispositions, instinctive drift) (PSY, BIO)	
	□ Observational Learning (PSY)	□ Modeling	
		□ Biological processes that affect observational learning	□ Mirror neurons □ Role of the brain in experiencing vicarious emotions
		□ Applications of observational learning to explain individual behavior	
	□ Theories of Attitude and Behavior Change (PSY)	□ Elaboration likelihood model	
		□ Social cognitive theory	
		□ Factors that affect attitude change (e.g., changing behavior, characteristics of the message and target, social factors)	
□ Foundational Concept 8: Psychological, sociocultural, and biological factors influence the way we think about ourselves and others, as well as how we interact with others.			
□ 8A. Self-identity	□ Self-Concept, Self-identity, and Social Identity (PSY, SOC)	□ The role of self-esteem, self-efficacy, and locus of control in self-concept and self-identity (PSY)	
		□ Different types of identities (e.g., race/ethnicity, gender, age, sexual orientation, class)	
	□ Formation of Identity (PSY, SOC)	□ Theories of identity development (e.g., gender, moral, psychosexual, social)	
		□ Influence of social factors on identity formation	□ Influence of individuals (e.g., imitation, looking-glass self, role-taking) □ Influence of groups (e.g., reference group)
		□ Influence of culture and socialization on identity formation	
□ 8B. Social thinking	□ Attributing Behavior to Persons or Situations (PSY)	□ Attributional processes (e.g., fundamental attribution error, role of culture in attributions)	
		□ How self-perceptions shape our perceptions of others	
		□ How perceptions of the environment shape our perceptions of others	
	□ Prejudice and Bias (PSY, SOC)	□ Processes that contribute to prejudice	□ Power, prestige, and class (SOC) □ The role of emotion in prejudice (PSY) □ The role of cognition in prejudice (PSY)
		□ Stereotypes	
		□ Stigma (SOC)	
		□ Ethnocentrism (SOC)	□ Ethnocentrism vs. cultural relativism
	□ Processes Related to Stereotypes (PSY)	□ Self-fulfilling prophecy	
		□ Stereotype threat	
□ 8C. Social interactions	□ Elements of Social Interaction (PSY, SOC)	□ Status (SOC)	□ Types of status (e.g., achieved, ascribed)
		□ Role	□ Role conflict and role strain (SOC) □ Role exit (SOC)
		□ Groups	□ Primary and secondary groups (SOC) □ In-group vs. out-group □ Group size (e.g., dyads, triads) (SOC)
		□ Networks (SOC)	

		□ Organizations (SOC)	□ Formal organization
			□ Bureaucracy
			  □ Characteristics of an ideal bureaucracy
			  □ Perspectives on bureaucracy (e.g., iron law of oligarchy, McDonaldization)

	□ Self-presentation and Interacting with Others (PSY, SOC)	□ Expressing and detecting emotion	□ The role of gender in the expression and detection of emotion □ The role of culture in the expression and detection of emotion
		□ Presentation of self	□ Impression management □ Front stage vs. back stage self (Dramaturgical approach) (SOC)
		□ Verbal and nonverbal communication	
		□ Animal signals and communication (PSY, BIO)	
	□ Social Behavior (PSY)	□ Attraction	
		□ Aggression	
		□ Attachment	
		□ Altruism	
		□ Social support (PSY, SOC)	
		□ Biological explanations of social behavior in animals (PSY, BIO)	□ Foraging behavior (BIO) □ Mating behavior and mate choice □ Applying game theory (BIO) □ Altruism □ Inclusive fitness (BIO)
	□ Discrimination (PSY, SOC)	□ Individual vs. institutional discrimination (SOC)	
		□ The relationship between prejudice and discrimination	
		□ How power, prestige, and class facilitate discrimination (SOC)	
□ Foundational Concept 9: Cultural and social differences influence well-being.			
□ 9A. Understanding social structure	□ Theoretical Approaches (SOC)	□ Microsociology vs. macrosociology	
		□ Functionalism	
		□ Conflict theory	
		□ Symbolic interactionism	
		□ Social constructionism	
		□ Exchange-rational choice	
		□ Feminist theory	
	□ Social Institutions (SOC)	□ Education	□ Hidden curriculum □ Teacher expectancy □ Educational segregation and stratification
		□ Family (PSY, SOC)	□ Forms of kinship (SOC) □ Diversity in family forms □ Marriage and divorce □ Violence in the family (e.g., child abuse, elder abuse, spousal abuse) (SOC)
		□ Religion	□ Religiosity □ Types of religious organizations (e.g., churches, sects, cults) □ Religion and social change (e.g., modernization, secularization, fundamentalism)
		□ Government and economy	□ Power and authority □ Comparative economic and political systems □ Division of labor
		□ Health and medicine	□ Medicalization □ The sick role □ Delivery of health care □ Illness experience □ Social epidemiology □

	□ Culture (PSY, SOC)	□ Elements of culture (e.g., beliefs, language, rituals, symbols, values)	
		□ Material vs. symbolic culture (SOC)	
		□ Culture lag (SOC)	
		□ Culture shock (SOC)	
		□ Assimilation (SOC)	
		□ Multiculturalism (SOC)	
		□ Subcultures and countercultures (SOC)	
		□ Mass media and popular culture (SOC)	
		□ Evolution and human culture (PSY, BIO)	
		□ Transmission and diffusion (SOC)	
□ **9B. Demographic characteristics and processes**	□ Demographic Structure of Society (PSY, SOC)	□ Age	□ Aging and the life course □ Age cohorts (SOC) □ Social significance of aging
		□ Gender	□ Sex versus gender □ The social construction of gender (SOC) □ Gender segregation (SOC)
		□ Race and ethnicity (SOC)	□ The social construction of race □ Racialization □ Racial formation
		□ Immigration status (SOC)	□ Patterns of immigration □ Intersections with race and ethnicity
		□ Sexual orientation	
	□ Demographic Shifts and Social Change (SOC)	□ Theories of demographic change (i.e., Malthusian theory and demographic transition)	
		□ Population growth and decline (e.g., population projections, population pyramids)	
		□ Fertility, migration, and mortality	□ Fertility and mortality rates (e.g., total, crude, age-specific) □ Patterns in fertility and mortality □ Push and pull factors in migration
		□ Social movements	□ Relative deprivation □ Organization of social movements □ Movement strategies and tactics
		□ Globalization	□ Factors contributing to globalization (e.g., communication technology, economic interdependence) □ Perspectives on globalization □ Social changes in globalization (e.g., civil unrest, terrorism)
		□ Urbanization	□ Industrialization and urban growth □ Suburbanization and urban decline □ Gentrification and urban renewal
□ Foundational Concept 10: Social stratification and access to resources influence well-being			
□ **10A. Social inequality**	□ Spatial Inequality (SOC)	□ Residential segregation	
		□ Neighborhood safety and violence	
		□ Environmental justice (location and exposure to health risks)	
	□ Social Class (SOC)	□ Aspects of social stratification	□ Social class and socioeconomic status □ Class consciousness and false consciousness □ Cultural capital and social capital □ Social reproduction □ Power, privilege, and prestige □ Intersectionality (e.g., race, gender, age) □ Socioeconomic gradient in health □ Global inequalities
		□ Patterns of social mobility	□ Intergenerational and intragenerational mobility □ Vertical and horizontal mobility □ Meritocracy
		□ Poverty	□ Relative and absolute poverty □ Social exclusion (segregation and isolation)
	□ Health Disparities (SOC) (e.g., class, gender, and race inequalities in health)		
	□ Healthcare Disparities (SOC) (e.g., class, gender, and race inequalities in health care)		

	Axilogy Early Medical Education Course Syllabus Outline		Use this outline to develop experience and knowledge prior to medical school.
Lesson	Biomedical Topic	Humanities Topic	Concept Review Method
1	Molecular Biology	Professionalism	
2	Cellular Biology	Patient Advocacy	
3	Back & Lower Limb Anatomy	Arts & Humanities	
4	Upper Limb Anatomy	Hidden Curriculum	
5	Thorax Anatomy	Learning & Memory	
6	Abdomen Anatomy	Safe Prescribing	
7	Pelvis Anatomy	Sleep	
8	Head & Neck Anatomy	Mid-Life & Death	
9	Neuroscience	Behavioral Neuroanatomy	
10	Genetics	History of Medicine	
11	Immunology	Elder Abuse	
12	Microbiology	Rural Healthcare	
13	Cardiovascular Physiology & Histology	Introduction To Public Health	
14	Respiratory Physiology & Histology	Medical Sociology	
15	Renal Physiology & Histology	Human Sexuality	
16	Gastrointestinal Biochemistry, Physiology, & Histology	Obesity and Eating Disorders	
17	Endocrine & Reproductive Functions	LGBTQIA Health	
18	Infectious Diseases	Global Healthcare	
19	Cardiovascular Pathology & Pharmacology	Public Health Research Analysis	
20	Pulmonary Pathology & Pharmacology	Smoking & Substance Misuse	
21	Rheumatology & Treatment	Biomedical Statistics	
22	Renal Pathology & Pharmacology	Online Research Portfolio	
23	Gastrointestinal Pathology & Pharmacology	Prevention: Exercise & Nutrition	
24	Neurology Diagnosis	Mental Disabilities	
25	Psychiatry Diagnosis	Major Depression	
26	Endocrinology Disease & Treatment	Behavioral Biochemistry	
27	Reproduction Pathology & Pharmacology	Prenatal- Preschool Development	
28	Hematology Disease & Treatment	Alcohol Misuse and Dependence	
29	Oncology Disease & Treatment	Biomedical Ethics & Laws	
30	Dermatology Disease & Treatment	Spirituality	
31	Internal Medicine	Health Care Disparities	
32	Surgery	Trauma Survivors	
33	Family Medicine	Disaster Management	
34	Obstetrics/ Gynecology	Toddler-Teen Development	
35	Psychiatry Disease & Treatment	Domestic & Child Abuse	
36	Neurology Disease & Treatment	Veteran Health	
37	Emergency Medicine	Homelessness	
38	Geriatrics	Homelessness	
39	Clinical Exams & Sports Medicine	Pain	
40	Team-Based Treatment	Practice Case Presentation	
41	USMLE content Review	Other	
42	Mock USMLE exam	Other	

49048951R00136

Made in the USA
San Bernardino, CA
11 May 2017